Department of the United States

Proclamations and decrees during the war with Spain

Department of the United States

Proclamations and decrees during the war with Spain

ISBN/EAN: 9783337231941

Printed in Europe, USA, Canada, Australia, Japan

Cover: Foto ©ninafisch / pixelio.de

More available books at **www.hansebooks.com**

THE WAR WITH SPAIN.

CONTENTS.

Proclamations and decrees of neutrality: Page.
- Argentine Republic.. 9
- Belgium.. 9
- Bermuda... 10
- Bolivia... 12
- Brazil.. 12
- British Guiana.. 17
- Canada... 17
- Cape of Good Hope... 17
- Ceylon.. 18
- China.. 18
- Costa Rica... 21
- Danish West Indies... 21
- Denmark... 23
- Dominican Republic... 24
- Dutch West Indies.. 26
- Ecuador... 29
- France... 29
- Germany... 30
- Gibraltar.. 30
- Great Britain... 31
- Greece... 37
- Guatemala... 38
- Haiti.. 38
- Italy... 41
- Jamaica... 44
- Japan... 46
- Korea... 49
- Leeward Islands.. 49
- Liberia... 49
- Malta... 50
- Mauritius... 50
- Mexico... 51
- Netherlands... 53
- Netherlands India... 57
- Nicaragua.. 59
- Paraguay... 59

Peru	60
Portugal	60
Roumania	62
Russia	63
Salvador	64
Servia	64
Siam	65
St. Lucia	65
Straits Settlements	65
Sweden and Norway	66
Switzerland	66
Turkey	67
Uruguay	67
Venezuela	68
Proclamations of the President of the United States	73
Orders of the War and Navy Departments:	
Occupation of Santiago	83
Instructions to blockading vessels and cruisers	85
War decrees of Spain	89

Introductory.

The following proclamations and decrees in regard to neutrality were issued by various governments shortly after the outbreak of hostilities between the United States and Spain in April, 1898. They have been, for the most part, printed from time to time in Advance Sheets of Consular Reports, and are published in this form, together with the war proclamations and decrees of the United States and Spain, for reference purposes.

Proclamations and Decrees of Neutrality.

Proclamations and Decrees of Neutrality.

ARGENTINE REPUBLIC.

Mr. François S. Jones, chargé d'affaires at Buenos Ayres, sends, under date of April 28, 1898, translation of a note from the Minister of Foreign Relations, as follows:

MINISTRY OF FOREIGN RELATIONS,
Buenos Ayres, April 27, 1898.

Mr. CHARGÉ D'AFFAIRES: I have had the honor to receive your note of yesterday's date by which, in compliance with orders from your Government, you are good enough to communicate to me that, in view of the joint resolution of the Congress of the United States, approved the 20th instant, directing intervention to secure the independence of the Island of Cuba, the Spanish Government informed the minister of the United States at Madrid on the following day that it considered the above-mentioned resolution equivalent to a declaration of war.

In taking cognizance of the deplorable circumstance which compromises the stability of two nations with which this Republic entertains the most cordial relations, His Excellency the President charges me to inform you, for communication to your Government, that he will at all times observe neutrality in accordance with the principles consecrated by international law.

Praying for the early termination of the war, I reiterate the assurances of my distinguished consideration.

A. ALCORTA.

BELGIUM.

Minister Storer sends from Brussels, under date of April 30, 1898, translation of an official statement by the Belgian Government (published in the Moniteur Belge, April 25 and 26, 1898), as follows:

OFFICIAL NOTICE.

Spain and the United States of America being in a state of war, the Government recalls to its citizens that Belgium is always neutral, and that every act against the obligations of neutrality must be carefully avoided.

The penal code contains the following section, to which the attention of the public should be called:

"ARTICLE 123. Whosoever by hostile proceedings, not approved by the Government, shall expose the State to (liability of) hostilities from any foreign power, shall be punished by imprisonment for from five to ten years; and should hostilities be the result, by imprisonment from ten to fifteen years."

BERMUDA.*

BERMUDA, ALIAS }
SOMERS' ISLANDS. }

[L. S. M.]
G. Digby Barker, Lieut.-General, Governor, and Commander in Chief.

By His Excellency George Digby Barker, Companion of the Most Honorable Order of the Bath, Lieutenant-General, Governor, Commander in Chief, and Ordinary in and over these Islands, etc.

A PROCLAMATION.

Whereas a state of war exists between Spain and the United States of America; and whereas I, the said governor and commander in chief, have received notification that it is Her Majesty's pleasure and command that a strict and impartial neutrality in the said state of war shall be maintained by all Her Majesty's subjects and all persons whatsoever entitled to Her protection; and

Whereas Her Majesty has been further pleased to command that six days from the day of the date of publication the following rules shall be in force:

RULES.

Rule A.—No ship of war of either belligerent may use British waters as place of resort for warlike purposes or equipment or may leave British waters until twenty-four hours after any ship of the other belligerent

Rule B.—Subject to Rule A, every such vessel of war shall be required to put to sea within twenty-four hours after entrance unless in the event of stress of weather or necessity for repair or provisioning, in which case she must leave as soon as possible and certainly within twenty-four hours of completion of repairs.

Rule C.—No supplies will be allowed beyond provisions and subsistence for crew necessary for immediate use and no coal beyond what will take the ship to the nearest port of her own country or nearest destination, nor will coal be supplied to the same ship in any British port twice within three months.

Rule D.—No prizes will be brought into British waters.

Now I, the said governor and commander in chief, do hereby warn all persons in this colony to take notice hereof, and do hereby proclaim that the aforesaid rules will take effect in this colony six days from the date hereof and are to be obeyed by all persons.

Given under my hand and the great seal of these islands, this 23d day of April, A. D. 1898, and in the sixty-first year of Her Majesty's reign.

By his excellency's command.

ARCHIBALD ALISON,
Colonial Secretary.

God save the Queen.

---

* Received May 2 from the United States consulate at Hamilton, Bermuda.

BERMUDA, ALIAS }
SOMERS' ISLANDS. }

[L. S. M.]
G. Digby Barker, Lieut.-
General, Governor, and
Commander in Chief.

By His Excellency George Digby Barker, Companion of the Most Honorable Order of the Bath, Lieutenant-General, Governor, Commander in Chief, and Ordinary in and over these Islands, etc.

A PROCLAMATION.

Whereas by a proclamation issued this day, I, the said governor and commander in chief, did proclaim that certain rules for the enforcement of neutrality in the state of war existing between Spain and the United States of America should come into force six days from the date thereof; and

Whereas Her Majesty has been pleased to command that such rules shall come into force forthwith:

Now I, the said governor and commander in chief, do hereby further proclaim that the said rules are now in force, of which all persons in this colony are directed to take notice and govern themselves accordingly.

Given under my hand and the great seal of these islands, this 23d day of April, A. D. 1898, and in the sixty-first year of Her Majesty's reign.

By his excellency's command.

ARCHIBALD ALISON,
Colonial Secretary.

God save the Queen.

COLONIAL SECRETARY'S OFFICE,
Hamilton, Bermuda, April 23, 1898.

With reference to the above proclamations, attention is drawn to the extract from the London Gazette published in a notification from this office dated the 24th May, 1897, which notification contains information respecting the requirements of the imperial act passed in the thirty-third and thirty-fourth year of Her Majesty's reign, entitled "An act to regulate the conduct of Her Majesty's subjects during the existence of hostilities between foreign states with which Her Majesty is at peace."

By his excellency's command.

ARCHIBALD ALISON,
Colonial Secretary.

Consul Greene, of Bermuda, sends, on May 6, 1898, copy of the following notice:

BERMUDA, ALIAS }
SOMERS' ISLANDS. }

[L. S. M.]
G. Digby Barker, Lieut.-
General, Governor, and
Commander in Chief.

By His Excellency George Digby Barker, Companion of the Most Honorable Order of the Bath, Lieutenant-General, Governor, Commander in Chief, and Ordinary in and over these Islands, etc.

A PROCLAMATION.

Whereas by a proclamation published on the 23d day of April, 1898, by me the said governor and commander in chief, certain rules made for the guidance of all persons in maintaining a strict and impartial neutrality in the state of war existing between Spain and the United States of America were declared to be in force in this colony; and

Whereas it is expedient to modify one of these rules:

Now I, the said governor and commander in chief, do hereby issue this my proclamation and do publish and declare that the following rule is substituted for Rule C as contained in the said previous proclamation:

Rule C.—No supplies will be allowed to any such ship beyond provisions and subsistence for crew necessary for immediate use and no coal except for the specific purpose (to be satisfactorily shown) of enabling her to proceed direct to the nearest port of her own country or other named nearer neutral destination, nor will coal be supplied to the same ship in any British port twice within three months.

Of which all persons in this colony are directed to take notice and govern themselves accordingly.

Given under my hand and the great seal of these islands this 6th day of May, A. D. 1898, and in the sixty-first year of Her Majesty's reign.

By his excellency's command.

God save the Queen.

ARCHIBALD ALISON,
Colonial Secretary.

BOLIVIA.

Minister Bridgman transmits from La Paz, under date of May 19, 1898, translation of a note from the Minister of Foreign Relations of Bolivia, as follows:

MINISTRY OF FOREIGN RELATIONS,
Sucre, May 11, 1898.

SIR: In response to your note of the 27th of April, I have the honor to announce to Your Excellency that the Government of Bolivia, deploring deeply the war which exists between the United States of America and the Kingdom of Spain, has kept from the first moment, and will continue to keep, the strictest neutrality in the said conflict.

I should have preferred to make this declaration personally to Your Excellency, but unfortunately the circumstances to which your note refers prevent me from so doing.

I renew, etc.,

M. M. GOMEZ.

BRAZIL.

Under date of April 29, 1898, Minister Bryan sends from Petropolis the following translation of a note from the Brazilian Minister of Foreign Affairs:

FOREIGN OFFICE,
Rio de Janeiro, April 27, 1898.

I have before me the note which Mr. Charles Page Bryan, envoy extraordinary and minister plenipotentiary of the United States of America, directed to me on the 26th instant, bringing to my attention the communication he had received from his

Government concerning the motive that had determined Congress to declare a state of war existing with Spain, beginning with the 21st day of this month.

His Excellency the President of the Republic, to whom I presented the said communication, regrets sincerely that the question which has caused the breaking off of diplomatic relations between the two countries could not have been solved by pacific means, and has charged me to declare that Brazil will observe the strictest neutrality during this war.

I have, etc.,

DIONISIO E. DE CASTRO CERQUEIRA.

The following circular, issued by the Brazilian Government for the guidance of the various departments, was sent by Mr. Bryan under date of May 5, 1898:

MINISTRY OF FOREIGN AFFAIRS,
Rio de Janeiro, April 29, 1898.

To the MINISTERS OF MARINE, WAR, JUSTICE, TREASURY, AND INDUSTRY.

Mr. MINISTERS: The legation of the United States of America, in the name of its Government, communicated to me on the 26th instant that the American Congress, by a joint resolution approved on the 20th, authorized the intervention of the said States to the end of securing the pacification and independence of the Island of Cuba, and that this resolution was considered a declaration of war by the Government of Spain, which ordered its legation to withdraw from Washington and interrupted diplomatic relations. Consequently, Congress declared that a state of war exists between the two nations, commencing the 21st. The President of the Republic, to whose knowledge I brought this communication, profoundly regretting that the question which caused the breaking off of relations between the two countries could not be solved by pacific means, determined that during this war Brazil would maintain the strictest neutrality, and, in order that this should be made effective, commands that the following regulations should be rigorously observed in all the territory of the Republic:

I.

Individuals residing in Brazil, citizens or foreigners, must abstain from all participation and aid in favor of either of the belligerents, and may not do any act which might be considered as hostile to either one of the two parties and, therefore, contrary to the obligations of neutrality.

II.

The Federal Government does not consent that privateers may be prepared or armed in the ports of the Republic.

III.

Neither belligerent will be permitted to promote enlistment in Brazil, not only of its own citizens, but also of the citizens of other countries, for the purpose of incorporating them with its forces of land and sea.

IV.

The exportation of material of war from the ports of Brazil to those of either of the belligerent powers, under the Brazilian flag, or that of any other nation, is absolutely prohibited.

V.

It is prohibited citizens or aliens residing in Brazil to announce by telegraph the departure or near arrival of any ship, merchant or war, of the belligerents, or to give to them any orders, instructions, or warnings, with the purpose of prejudicing the enemy.

VI.

No war ship or privateer shall be permitted to enter and remain, with prizes, in our ports or bays during more than twenty-four hours, except in case of a forced putting into port, and in no manner shall it be permitted to it to dispose of its prizes or of articles coming out of them.

By the words "except in case of a forced putting into port" should also be understood that a ship shall not be required to leave port within the said time :

First. If it shall not have been able to make the preparations indispensable to enable it to go to sea without risk of being lost.

Second. If there should be the same risk on account of bad weather.

Third. And, finally, if it should be menaced by an enemy.

In these cases, it shall be for the Government, at its discretion, to determine, in view of the circumstances, the time within which the ship should leave.

VII.

Privateers, although they do not conduct prizes, shall not be admitted to the ports of the Republic for more than twenty-four hours, except in the cases indicated in the preceding section.

VIII.

No ship with the flag of one of the belligerents, employed in the war, or destined for the same, may be provisioned, equipped, or armed in the ports of the Republic, the furnishing of victuals and naval stores which it may absolutely need and the things indispensable for the continuation of its voyage not being included in this prohibition.

IX.

The last provision of the preceding section presupposes that the ship is bound for a certain port, and that it is only en route and puts into a port of the Republic through stress of circumstances. This, moreover, will not be considered as verified if the same ship tries the same port repeated times, or after having been relieved in one port should subsequently enter another, under the same pretext, except in proven cases of compelling circumstances. Therefore, repeated visits without a sufficiently justified motive would authorize the suspicion that the ship is not really en route, but is frequenting the seas near Brazil in order to make prizes of hostile ships. In such cases, asylum or succor given to a ship would be characterized as assistance or favor given against the other belligerent, being thus a breach of neutrality.

Therefore, a ship which shall once have entered one of our ports shall not be received in that or another shortly after having left the first, in order to take victuals, naval stores, or make repairs, except in a duly proved case of compelling circumstances, unless after a reasonable interval which would make it seem probable that the ship had left the coast of Brazil and had returned after having finished the voyage she was undertaking.

X.

The movements of the belligerent will be under the supervision of the customs authorities from the time of entrance until that of departure, for the purpose of verifying the proper character of the things put on board.

XI.

The ships of belligerents shall take material for combustion only for the continuance of their voyage.

Furnishing coal to ships which sail the seas near Brazil for the purpose of making prizes of an enemy's vessels or prosecuting any other kind of hostile operations is prohibited.

A ship which shall have once received material for combustion in our ports shall not be allowed a new supply there, unless there shall have elapsed a reasonable interval which makes it probable that said ship has returned after having finished its voyage to a foreign port.

XII.

It will not be permitted to either of the belligerents to receive in the ports of the Republic goods coming directly for them in the ships of any nation whatever.

This means that the belligerents may not seek ports en route and on account of an unforeseen necessity, while having the intention of remaining in the vicinity of the coasts of Brazil, taking thus beforehand the necessary precautions to furnish themselves with the means of continuing their enterprises. The tolerance of such an abuse would be equivalent to allowing our ports to serve as a base of operations for the belligerents.

XIII.

The belligerents will not be permitted in the ports of Brazil—

First. To increase their crews, hiring seamen of any nationality whatsoever, including their own citizens.

Second. To increase the number and the caliber of their artillery, or by any means to perfect it; to buy or embark small arms or munitions of war.

There will be indicated to them an anchorage where they shall be under the immediate observation of the police, far from suspected places and circumstances.

XIV.

The belligerents, while they remain in the ports of the Republic, shall be forbidden—

To employ force or stratagem to recover prizes made from their fellow-citizens, or which may be made in the same harbor, or to liberate prisoners of their nation.

To undertake the sale or ransom of prizes made from the enemy before the validity of the prize shall have been recognized by competent courts.

To dispose of things taken from prizes they have on board.

XV.

The ships of either of the belligerents, however, which may be admitted to anchorage or harbor in the Republic, must remain in perfect quiet and complete peace with all the ships which may be there, especially those of war or armed for war, belonging to the hostile power.

The Brazilian forts and war ships will be ordered to fire upon a ship which shall attack its enemy within Brazilian harbors or territorial waters.

XVI.

No ship shall be allowed to leave port immediately after a ship belonging to a hostile nation or a neutral nation.

If the vessel leaving, as well as that left behind, be a steamer, or both be sailing vessels, there shall remain the interval of twenty-four hours between the sailing of

Merchant ships of one of the belligerents which may wish to leave port must give advice, in writing, twenty-four hours in advance to the commandant of the naval station of the day and hour for weighing anchor. In this advice shall be a statement whether they are steam or sail.

The commandant of the naval station, if he shall not have been advised of the departure of any war ship of the other belligerent shall send and inform the respective commanders that they may leave port only after the expiration of the time fixed in the preceding number. He shall give, besides this, the requisite advices to the forts and Government ships.

Merchant ships may not weigh anchor unless they have had an answer in writing declaring that the necessary measures have been taken and that therefore they may leave. The answer will be given with great promptness. In places where there is no commandant of the naval station, the advice of merchant ships shall be directed to the port captain; in default of this, to the commander of the Government fort; if there is no fort, to any Brazilian war ship which may be there.

The official to whom the advice, in the aforesaid terms, shall be directed is the authorized person to give the warning to belligerent war ships.

XVIII.

Belligerent war ships which shall not wish to have their departure impeded by the successive leaving of merchant vessels or hostile war ships should communicate twenty-four hours in advance, to one of the officials indicated in the preceding section and who shall be the authorized person on the occasion, an application for leaving. Priority of sailing will be determined by the receipt of advice.

XIX.

War ships may not leave port unless the merchant vessels of the other belligerent which may be at the bar or have been announced by telegraph or other means first enter, except the respective commanders give their word of honor to the commandant of the naval station, and, in default of him, to the authorized official, that they will do no harm to them; and if, besides this, they shall not be prevented by some other reason.

XX.

Neither of the belligerents may take prizes in the territorial waters of Brazil, or place themselves in ambuscade in the ports or anchorages, islands, or capes situated in those waters, to watch for hostile ships coming in or going out; try to get information in regard to those which are expected, or are to go out, or finally, to make sail to chase a hostile ship sighted or signaled.

All necessary means, including force, will be employed to prevent prize taking in territorial waters.

XXI.

If prizes brought to the ports of the Republic shall have been taken in territorial waters, the things coming out of them shall be taken possession of by the competent authorities, in order to restore them to their lawful owners, the sale of such things being always taken and considered as void.

XXII.

Ships which shall try to violate neutrality shall be immediately warned to leave the maritime jurisdiction of Brazil, and nothing shall be furnished them.

The belligerent who shall infringe the requirements of this circular shall be no more admitted into the ports of Brazil.

XXIII.

For the repression of violations which may be made, force shall be employed and, in default or insufficiency of that, protest shall be made against the belligerent that, advised and warned, shall not have desisted from violating the neutrality of Brazil, knowledge of the fact being immediately given to the Federal Government, with which the competent authorities should communicate by telegraph in cases not provided for herein.

I ask of you the speedy sending of orders that this circular be faithfully observed by each ministry, in those parts which refer to it, by the authorities subordinate to it.

Greeting.   DIONISIO E. DE CASTRO CERQUEIRA.

BRITISH GUIANA.

Consul Moulton, of Demerara, incloses, under date of May 4, 1898, a copy of the Georgetown Chronicle of April 26, 1898, containing the proclamation of neutrality by the governor of British Guiana. The proclamation, after the formal preamble, quotes the terms of the act in regard to the conduct of British subjects and of the rules governing ships of belligerents given in the proclamation of neutrality of Great Britain.*

CANADA.

Under date of April 29, 1898, Consul-General Turner sends from Ottawa copy of the Canada Gazette, of April 28, containing the proclamation of neutrality in French and English. The proclamation is in the same terms, mutatis mutandis, as that of Great Britain,* except as to preamble.

CAPE OF GOOD HOPE.

Consul-General Stowe sends from Cape Town, under date of May 26, 1898, copy of the proclamation of the governor of the colony, dated April 25, 1898, in regard to the observance of neutrality. The proclamation, after the usual preamble, quotes the rules in regard to illegal enlistment and shipbuilding and the use of British ports by vessels of belligerents which were published in the proclamation of neutrality by Great Britain.*

*See p. 31.

CEYLON.

Consul Morey sends from Colombo, under date of April 26, 1898, copy of the Ceylon Government Gazette Extraordinary, of April 25, 1898, containing the following:

GOVERNMENT NOTIFICATION.

War having unhappily broken out between Spain and the United States of America, his excellency the governor hereby strictly charges and commands all British subjects and other persons within the Island of Ceylon and its dependencies to observe the strictest and most impartial neutrality between the belligerents.

His excellency further calls the attention and desires the obedience of all persons to the requirements of the foreign enlistment act and of the following rules, which were published on two similar occasions in the Ceylon Government Gazette Extraordinary of the 30th August, 1894, and of the 29th May, 1897, and which, mutatis mutandis, shall forthwith apply to the present state of hostilities between Spain and the United States of America.

By his excellency's command.
E. NOEL WALKER,
Colonial Secretary.
COLONIAL SECRETARY'S OFFICE, *Colombo, April 25, 1898.*

The terms of the act in regard to the conduct of British subjects, and the rules governing ships of belligerents—as given in the proclamation of neutrality of Great Britain*—follow.

CHINA.

Minister Denby sends the following from Pekin, under date of May 2, 1898:

The Tsungli Yamén to Mr. Denby.

PEKIN, *May 2, 1898.*

YOUR EXCELLENCY: The Princes and Ministers have had the honor to receive a communication from the minister of the United States, stating that the Congress of the United States passed on the 20th of April a joint resolution directing intervention for the pacification and independence of Cuba. The Government of Spain on the 21st instant informed the minister of the United States at Madrid that it considered this resolution equivalent to a declaration of war, and that it had accordingly withdrawn its minister from Washington and terminated all diplomatic relations with the United States.

The Congress of the United States thereupon, by an act approved the 26th of April, declared that a state of war exists between the two countries since and including the 21st of April.

The minister of the United States is directed by his Government to give this information to the Princes and Ministers, so that the neutrality of the Empire of China may be assured in the existing war.

In reply, the Princes and Ministers have to observe that the Government of China will duly maintain the laws of neutrality. The Yamén have therefore tele-

---
* See p. 31.

graphed the viceroys, governors, and tartar-generals of the Yangtze and maritime provinces to issue instructions to their subordinates that they are to observe the laws of neutrality. Further, instructions have been issued to the high authorities of all the provinces and to the inspector-general of customs to issue proclamations for general information.

The Princes and Ministers have the honor to send this reply for the information of the minister of the United States.

Minister Denby transmits, under date of May 17, the following note:

The Tsungli Yamên to Mr. Denby.

No. 10.] PEKIN, *May 9, 1898.*

YOUR EXCELLENCY: The Princes and Ministers have had the honor to receive a communication from the minister of the United States, announcing the fact that hostilities had commenced between the Government of the United States and the Government of Spain, and requesting that the neutrality of the Empire of China may be assured in the existing war.

On the 2d of May the Yamên telegraphed to the viceroys, governors, and tartar-generals of the various provinces to observe the laws of neutrality. Further, instructions were issued to the high authorities of all the provinces and to the inspector-general of customs to issue proclamations for general information. The Yamên duly informed the United States minister of the action taken by the Chinese Government as above. A decree has now been issued by the Emperor to the following effect:

"As war exists between the United States and Spain, it is right that China should observe the laws of neutrality. Severe injunctions must therefore be issued that no assistance to either of the belligerent powers shall be rendered by China. War vessels of either of the belligerent powers can not remain in Chinese ports, thus maintaining the rules of international law. Orders are therefore issued to take action accordingly."

The Yamên have therefore telegraphed the above decree to the Minister Superintendent of Southern and Northern Trade, and, as in duty bound, the Princes and Ministers send this communication for the information of the minister of the United States, asking him to telegraph to his Government that, as war exists between the United States and Spain, war vessels of either of the belligerent powers can not anchor in Chinese ports, in due observance of international law.

The Department has received the following from Consul-General Goodnow, dated Shanghai, May 22, 1898:

I have the honor to send herewith the "proclamation for the observance of international law," issued by the taotai of Shanghai, together with a translation thereof:

The translation reads:

PROCLAMATION FOR OBSERVANCE OF INTERNATIONAL LAW.

Tsai, taotai of Shanghai, in obedience to the imperial command, issues this proclamation:

We Chinese have during the past years been at peace with the United States and Spain. Just now these two nations are at war. We Chinese must observe the laws of strict neutrality, and must not furnish supplies of war to the two nations, nor interfere with present peaceful relations with either. We must not disobey international law. We ought to be more than careful to preserve friendship with citizens of both countries dwelling in. this country; and our citizens residing in countries under jurisdiction of United States and Spain, doing business and having protection of said Governments, also must be careful not to violate international law; and until these two countries are restored to the blessings of peace you at home and abroad must avoid any concern with the warfare between them, lest you bring evil upon yourselves.

I, the taotai of this port, in obedience to the Tsungli Yamên, who have petitioned the Throne and have sent a telegram ordering me to issue a proclamation informing the people, respectfully obey this command and issue this proclamation for the information of the people residing in our country's seas, roads, harbors, thoroughfares, water ways, ports, and branch creeks under the control of the Chinese Government that, as the United States and Spain are now at war, they (the people) ought to obey the following regulations:

(1) The war ships of the two nations must not use Chinese-controlled waters and ports for anchorage or fighting purposes, or anchor there for lading war supplies. If the merchant or war ship of one belligerent leave a Chinese port, a ship of the other must not be permitted to leave within twenty-four hours afterwards.

(2) After issuance of this proclamation, should any war ship of either belligerent come into a Chinese port, except on account of heavy winds or storms or to obtain food for crew or for repairs, it must not remain over twenty-four hours, and the officials in charge of the port or water way must, at the end of twenty-four hours, compel said boat to leave, and must not permit the loading of more provisions than are actually needed by the crew. In case of repairs, the ship must leave within twenty-four hours after repairs are completed. No delay must be permitted. War or merchant ships, of whichever nation, in a Chinese port, must be separated in leaving by twenty-four hours' time, and must not leave before or remain longer than said time.

(3) Hereafter the ships of the two nations in ports or water ways of China must not take on a large amount of provisions or supplies. In provisions the amount must be regulated by the needs of the number of men aboard; in coal, only sufficient must be allowed to take it to its nearest port, and it must not return for coaling more than once in three months.

(4) War ships of either party must not bring goods taken in battle into Chinese ports. Our people must not use their own boats secretly to furnish food or war supplies to the belligerents. Chinese in places governed by foreigners also must not secretly assist them in war. After issue of this proclamation, if you dare to disobey this command and not observe the duties of neutrals, or presume to disobey laws of nations and enter or cross their lines of blockade by sending men, dispatches, weapons, or any other contraband material for making supplies, you will find that you have put your head in the net of the law. Not only will I not protect you, but will most surely punish without mercy. Let all carefully observe and not disobey.

COSTA RICA.

Under date of May 14, 1898, Minister Merry sends the following from San José:

OFFICE OF FOREIGN RELATIONS,
San José, May 14, 1898.

Mr. MINISTER: The estimable note of Your Excellency has been received, dated the 11th instant, in which, by order of your Government, you communicate to mine officially the existence of a state of war between the United States and Spain. With the same note Your Excellency has been pleased to send to this office a printed copy of the decree ordered by Mr. President McKinley on the 26th of April last, and also a printed copy of the correspondence passed between the cabinets of Washington and Madrid on the 21st of said month and days immediately preceding.

By instructions of the President, I have the honor to assure Your Excellency in reply that this Government, deploring that the United States and Spain, nations with which Costa Rica has cultivated and now cultivates relations of the most intimate friendship, have seen the painful necessity to have recourse to the arbitrament of arms to settle their differences, and that this Republic being, and not able to be less than, neutral, will comply strictly with the duties which as such it should observe.

Your Excellency will accept, etc.,

P. PEREZ ZELEDON.

DANISH WEST INDIES.

Consul Van Horne sends from St. Thomas, under date of June 2, 1898, clippings from the St. Thomæ Tidende of May 21, in which the following announcements appear:

[Translation.]

WE CHRISTIAN THE NINTH,

By the grace of God King of Denmark, the Vandals and the Goths, Duke of Slesvig, Holstein, Stormarn, Ditmarsken, Lauenborg, and Oldenborg.

Make known: That whereas, under existing circumstances it is of importance that Danish subjects do not commit any act endangering the neutrality of the State or giving foreign powers reasonable grounds of complaint of the Danish State as a neutral power, we have found it urgently necessary, in accordance with the twenty-fifth section of the fundamental law, by provisional law to provide needful legal warrant for prohibiting and, in cases of transgression, punishing such acts in the Kingdom and in the Danish West India Islands.

To that end we require and command as follows:

SECTION 1. In the event of the outbreak of a war in which the Danish State is neutral, the subjects are prohibited—

(1) To take service in any quality soever in the army of the belligerent powers or on board their government ships, such prohibition to include piloting their ships of war or transport outside the reach of Danish pilotage, or, except in case of danger of the sea, assisting them in sailing the ship.

(2) To build or remodel, sell or otherwise convey, directly or indirectly, for or to any of the belligerent powers, ships known or supposed to be intended for any

purposes of war, or to cooperate in any manner on or from Danish territory in the arming or fitting out of such ships for enterprises of war.

(3) On or from Danish territory to assist any of the belligerent powers in their enterprises of war, such as supplying their ships with articles that must be considered as contraband of war, or carrying on for any of the belligerent powers work tending to increase the armament of their ships, or otherwise enhance the strength or mobility of such ships for purposes of war.

(4) To transport contraband of war for any of the belligerent powers, or hire or charter to them ships known or supposed to be intended for such use.

(5) To publicly request any person or persons to join the army or navy of the belligerent powers, or otherwise afford them assistance in carrying on the war; and, in case that the Government has issued special prohibition against so doing, to publicly invite to participation in the floating of state loans to any of the belligerent powers.

SEC. 2. Transgression of the above enactments is punished, in so far as no higher penalty is prescribed by law, with imprisonment or fines. Cases of participation and attempt will, in the Kingdom, be dealt with in accordance with the principles of the civil penal law; in the Danish West India Islands the principles of the general penal legislation become applicable.

The present law takes effect in the Kingdom at once.

With which all concerned have to comply.

Given at Amalienborg, the 29th of April, 1898, under our royal hand and seal.

CHRISTIAN R. [L. S.]

PUBLICATION FOR THE DANISH WEST INDIA ISLANDS WITH REFERENCE TO THE WAR EXISTING BETWEEN THE UNITED STATES OF NORTH AMERICA AND SPAIN.

For the information of Danish West India merchants and shipmasters in respect of their duty and position under general legislation and international law during the war between the United States and Spain, the following directions are by command of His Majesty the King published and enjoined:

SECTION 1. When a Danish West India merchant ship is on the sea hailed or stopped by any belligerent ship of war or authorized privateer, such ship shall, on the demand of the commanding officer, without fail present the ship's papers prescribed by section 2 of the registration ordinance, to wit: The certificate of nationality and registration, the ship's muster roll, clearance certificate, and cargo papers. Under international law, no vessel must be provided with a double set of ship's papers or carry any other flag than the flag of the country to which she belongs.

SEC. 2. Notwithstanding that neither of the belligerent powers have acceded to the Paris declaration of the 16th of April, 1856, both parties have expressed themselves officially to the effect that they recognize that the neutral flag covers the cargo, with the exception of contraband of war, and that neutral cargo, with the exception of contraband of war, in the enemy's ship is not subject to seizure. As contraband of war the following are considered: Arms, ammunition, articles of clothing and accouterment, and other articles manufactured and immediately applicable for and to purposes of war, in so far as they are intended for any of the belligerent powers or their subjects. Furthermore, dispatches from or to any of the governmental authorities of any of the belligerent powers are liable to be considered as contraband of war, which it is forbidden to carry. In case that alterations or additional rules in respect of contraband of war should become necessary, the Ministry of Finances will make such further publication as shall be required.

SEC. 3. It is the shipmaster's duty to inform himself as far as possible as to whether the belligerent port to which he is destined is blockaded. If, while going to enter a port the blockade of which was unknown to him, he is hailed or stopped by a ship of war belonging to the other belligerent power and the commanding officer informs him that the port is blockaded, it is his duty to withdraw at once, without attempting to enter the port secretly.

SEC. 4. If a shipmaster considers himself justified in complaining of the action in his case of any belligerent armed vessel, he must as soon as possible apply with his reclamation to the governor of the Danish West India Islands, or to the Ministry of Foreign Affairs, or to a royal Danish embassy or consulate.

HÖRRING.

The MINISTRY OF FINANCES, *May 2, 1898.*

DENMARK.

A note received by the Department from the Danish legation, under date of May 14, 1898, says:

The Danish Government announces that, desiring to conserve its relations of friendship and good understanding with the two belligerent parties, it will observe during the present war between Spain and the United States a strict and impartial neutrality; and for the purpose of preventing the Danish Antilles from becoming a base of military operations, contrary to the laws of neutrality, the Government of the King deems it his duty to announce beforehand to the parties belligerent the conditions under which their vessels of war will be permitted to enter and sojourn in the territorial waters of the Danish Antilles.

First. Vessels of war of either belligerent or transport boats belonging to their fleets will be permitted to enter the ports and territorial waters of the islands, but to remain there only during twenty-four hours, except in case they find themselves in distress caused either by bad weather, lack of provisions, accident or other cause. The sojourn of twenty-four hours will be counted from the moment when the cause of distress shall have ceased to exist and the necessary repairs or replenishment of stores have been made. An interval of twenty-four hours should in all cases intervene between the time of departure of the war ship or merchantman of one of the belligerent parties and the departure of a war ship of the other. Privateers will not be admitted into the ports or territorial waters except in case of manifest distress.

Second. Vessels belonging to the fleets of the belligerent parties will be permitted to provide themselves in the ports and territorial waters, with all necessaries and merchandise of which they may have need, with the exception of articles which are contraband of war. Nevertheless, they shall not be able to provision themselves beyond the quantity necessary for the use of the vessel's crew, nor to take coal in greater quantity than is necessary to enable the vessel to arrive at the nearest port of its own country or to some other destination nearer by. This privilege of coaling in a port or in the territorial waters of the islands shall be accorded to the same vessel only once in three months, except in case of special authorization of the governor.

Third. The ports and territorial waters of the islands shall be closed to the prizes of either belligerent, except when they are found in cases of distress.

DOMINICAN REPUBLIC.

Consul Grimke sends from Santo Domingo, under date of May 11, 1898, copy of the proclamation by President Heureaux in regard to the neutrality of the country, as follows:

The United States and Spain are in a state of war, and, as this formidable struggle, which must take place principally in our vicinity, will interfere, at least temporarily, with the business of the Republic, it becomes my duty, in my capacity as First Magistrate of the nation, to lay down rules for the guidance of the people from whom I hold so great responsibility.

First, I must counsel my fellow-citizens to observe the strictest neutrality in the war which has commenced. Our international duties, the good faith due to the northern Republic and to its citizens impose this upon us. The friend of both combatants, it would be treachery if, while expressing cordial sentiments, we should, secretly or openly, favor one party to the inevitable injury of the other. We must confine ourselves to deploring sincerely that two friendly peoples have been unable to find a peaceful solution of the differences which divide them, and that compelled by circumstances to appeal to arms, the blood of their sons, which we would wish to spare, must flow in abundance, and the wealth, laboriously accumulated in times of peace, be dissipated.

The people of the Dominican Republic should be before all and above all Dominicans. The interests of their country should take precedence above all others, a national ideal should ever inspire their acts and thoughts. * * *

Our own security, the danger to which we would be exposed by compromising ourselves with either of the two nations, endowed with forces so greatly superior to our own, compels us to be neutral, absolutely neutral, between Spain and the United States. Justice and good faith are our safeguards, and it would be imprudent to separate ourselves voluntarily from them and to enter the lists without the only arms capable of protecting us.

By preserving strict neutrality, we can succeed in avoiding the gravest contingencies of the bloody conflict, but we can not succeed in protecting ourselves from its fatal economic consequences. Misfortune can not knock at our neighbor's door without bequeathing to us a portion of the sorrow it brings. The close ties which progress establishes between civilized nations make tolerance and prosperity common property. The wound which bleeds the one exhausts both. I wish to call attention to these consequences of the war, unfortunately inevitable, that, knowing the causes, public opinion may not be misled, and that precious time may not be lost studying the situation from a false point of view and searching for relief where it can not be found. The first injurious result for us, one already experienced, is the reducing of credits, by which commercial interests are affected, resources depreciated, the sphere of action limited, and serious perturbation produced. Capital is timid, and at the first intimation of war everyone who could withdraw his money from the hazardous circulation of the times did so, reducing by so much the quantity available. The natural result is, that the credits to Dominican merchants are reduced in the same proportion; everyone who has not ready money with which to make his purchases in the producing markets meets with loss, equilibrium being shaken at the very time when it is most difficult, on account of the natural fear of the capitalists in our markets, to find the funds needful to continue business with the same freedom as before.

On the other hand, the transportation and the sale of our fruits has become difficult while the war lasts, costs and risks being increased and profits diminished. Thus, the amount which the country annually spends for its purchases in foreign lands being diminished, exchange is higher than usual. The price of everything has increased and will continue to increase. The scarcity of the most necessary articles has begun to be felt and will be accentuated, if our people do not display the courage that circumstances demand. The provisioning of our markets can not, perhaps, be accomplished with the usual regularity; and, even if this adverse possibility were met, another more serious and more difficult to be overcome will remain in existence. The United States, our principal granary, is organizing a great army, for which the Government will be compelled to provide enormous quantities of provisions, reducing in this manner the quantity offered for export and causing an advance in the prices. In our land, prices have already increased and will continue to rise, so that the laboring classes will suffer painful privations, the scarcity of food occurring at the same time as the reduction of the circulating medium, together with the decrease of occupation in export enterprises.

On account of the urgent needs, for the sake of our national honor, that we may not have the shame of suffering want in time of peace for lack of the grains and fruits which our soil produces with such liberality, I beg and entreat our agriculturists to devote themselves to the cultivation of small fruits, to confide to the generous bosom of the earth, not only the capital they possess, but the fate and destiny of their country, seriously menaced by famine. Grains, potatoes, etc., that are easily preserved and yield an abundant yearly harvest, will repay with interest the labor devoted to their cultivation, and will save the country from suffering caused by lack of foresight and industry. The circular of the Minister of the Interior should receive the attention of everyone; and to the governors and municipal heads, I especially recommend the reading and carrying out of his directions. Let us search with earnestness and intelligence for the remedy for the evils threatening us, and cease useless lamentations for misfortunes that man can not avert.

With the preservation and advancement of the Republic, civilized, united, and self-governed as our sole ideal, we invoke the patriotism of our citizens to supply the calm and good sense necessary to permanent, absolute neutrality. The gravity of the situation, our national interests, the necessities of the hour, should inspire us, and wisdom and prudence will indicate the means of preventing misery, of producing the food we consume, of becoming our own providers. Our soil is capable of yielding an abundant harvest of rice, corn, beans, and potatoes, articles which to-day come to us from abroad. Thus, we will not only prevent present want, but will save ourselves from even greater misfortunes. Times of hardship are the ones chosen by revolutionists for their wicked propaganda, as the mind of the people is then most ready to receive impressions. There is a fatal tendency in the heart of man to make someone responsible for his misfortunes, attributing them to fate or to some individual who, perhaps, did his best to avoid them. In the interests of our country let us reflect upon these observations. The Republic enjoys the most complete peace; under its protection obvious progress has been made, and the Government has prepared itself to meet any emergency that may arise; and to its beneficent influence, the civil and political authorities owe the union of force and good will so necessary to the success of all undertakings entrusted to them. If, unfortunately, peace should be broken, the Government relies on all the necessary elements to reestablish it; but it would profoundly regret being obliged to exercise repressive action at the very time when its greatest anxiety is to favor all with its paternal aid. The most discreet, the most patriotic part is to maintain the tranquillity which the situation demands, to place our hearts, full of love for our country, at the service of reason, which must guide us in saving the Republic and making it prosperous. Thus, we will succeed in conducting the affairs of state with prudence and skill that will reflect credit on a people which possesses such qualities, and uses them at the critical hour when other states show their lack of calm and good sense. Labor in all its forms, agricultural labor especially, is our salvation. Let us place our trust, our energy, our perseverance in this, and, with the impetus that it gives to production, we will gain the great advantage of changing the position of our State from dependence to independence, providing the provisions the lack of which to-day exposes us to such misfortune.

U. HEUREAUX.

SANTO DOMINGO, *May 5, 1898.*

DUTCH WEST INDIES.

Under date of May 12, 1898, Consul Smith sends from Curaçao a copy of the official journal, De Curaçaosche Courant, of May 6, containing a notification in regard to the attitude of the inhabitants during the war, which is translated as follows:

[Translation.]

WARNING.

GOVERNMENT SECRETARY'S OFFICE,
Curaçao, May 3, 1898.

In view of the breaking out of the war between Spain and the United States of America, all inhabitants are warned, in the name of the governor of the colony, to engage in no manner whatever in the sale or exchange of, or other transactions with, prizes; to furnish no assistance or material for repairing men-of-war or privateers of the above-named nations; to take no part in equipping vessels presumptively destined for war or privateer service; and they are at the same time warned for their own interest not to deliver coal to such vessels without the knowledge of the governor.

The Government's Secretary,
HELLMUND.

The publication sheets issued by the Dutch West Indies, referring to transshipment of war materials and containing the rules of neutrality to be observed in the war between the United States and Spain, were sent by Consul Smith on June 20, 1898.

Translations are as follows:

1898. No. 9.
PUBLICATION SHEET.

Ordinance supplementing article 20 of the ordinance of July 28–December 20, 1881, "containing an amendment of the regulations in force concerning the importation, transit, and exportation of merchandise in the Island of Curaçao, and the proof of the collection of the fire and light-house dues there." (Publication Sheet No. 22.)

In the Queen's name: The governor of Curaçao, considering that it is necessary to supplement article 20 of the ordinance of July 28–December 20, 1881, "containing an amendment of the regulations in force concerning the importation, transit, and exportation of merchandise in the Island of Curaçao, and the proof of the collection of the fire and light-house dues there" (Publication Sheet No. 22), has, with the approbation of the colonial council, and by virtue of the second section of article 50 of the governmental regulations of this colony, decreed the following ordinance:

ARTICLE I. The following is added to article 20 of the ordinance of July 28–December 20, 1881 (Publication Sheet No. 22), as a sixth paragraph:

"The transshipment of gunpowder, ammunition, firearms, side arms, or other war materials may be prohibited from time to time by decree of the governor."

ART. 2. This ordinance goes into effect on the day of its promulgation.

Given at Willemstad, June 4, 1898.

BARGE.

Promulgated, June 4, 1898.

HELLMUND, *Secretary*.

1898.   No. 11.

PUBLICATION SHEET.—PUBLICATION.

The governor of Curaçao, in view of the report of His Excellency, the Minister of the Colonies, of May 24 of this year, hereby notifies all whom it may concern that, for the maintenance and exercise of a complete neutrality during the war which has arisen between powers in friendship with us, Spain on the one side and the United States of America on the other, the following regulations are decreed:

ARTICLE I. It is forbidden to furnish the war vessels or privateers of the belligerents with arms or ammunition, or to assist them in any manner in increasing their crews, arms, or armament, and, generally, to perform intentionally any act by which the neutrality of the State may be endangered.

ART. 2. Are likewise prohibited:

(*a*) The fitting out in the colony of vessels of war or other vessels intended for military purposes, for the use of the belligerents, or to furnish or sell such vessels to the said parties.

(*b*) The exportation of arms, ammunition, or other war materials to the belligerents. This includes the exportation of everything that is adapted to immediate use in war, but not unmanufactured materials, provided they are not generally used for military purposes.

(*c*) The enlistment of soldiers or seamen for the belligerents within the territory of the colony.

(*d*) The organization in a military manner, in the territory of the colony, of volunteers, with the intent to proceed thence to the camp of either of the belligerents.

The governor further calls attention to articles 54 and 55 of the criminal code, and warns all the inhabitants of the colony not to engage in any manner in privateering, and not to take out any foreign letters of marque, as those who engage in privateering in such manner, or lend their aid thereto, will be prosecuted before the courts.

The governor likewise calls the attention of the masters, owners, and freighters of vessels to the danger and losses to which they will expose themselves by failing, in violation of the duties imposed upon neutral powers, to respect an effective blockade, or by carrying contraband of war or military dispatches for either of the belligerents.

Those rendering themselves guilty of such acts will be liable to all the consequences arising therefrom, and can not count upon any protection whatever through the intervention of Her Majesty's Government.

BARGE, *Governor*

WILLEMSTAD, *June 17, 1898*.

PUBLICATION SHEET.—PUBLICATION.

The governor of Curaçao, in view of the report of May 24 of this year of the Minister of the Colonies, notifies all whom it may concern that, for the observance and exercise of a complete neutrality during the war which has arisen between powers in friendship with us, Spain on the one side and the United States of America on the other, the following regulations are decreed:

ARTICLE 1. Ships and vessels of war of the belligerents will be admitted to the harbors and roadsteads of the colony for a stay of twenty-four hours at most, unless it is shown to be necessary to grant them a longer stay to enable them to provide themselves with provisions or coal, or in cases of distress or dangers of the sea. In such cases, however, they must depart as soon as they have finished taking in provisions or coal, within the first twenty-four hours, if possible; otherwise, as quickly as practicable, as soon as the danger is past, and in the case of repairs, within twenty-four hours, at the furthest, after the repairs have been finished. The period of twenty-four hours at the utmost fixed for the stay in port shall be exceeded only when necessary to the execution of the provisions of article 5 of this publication. Such quantity of provisions may be taken on board as is sufficient for the subsistence of the crew, but the supply of coal must not be more than sufficient to enable the ship or vessel to reach the nearest port of the country to which it belongs, or that of one of its allies in the war. The same vessel shall not be supplied a second time with coal until at least three months have elapsed since the former supply, unless special permission be granted to that effect.

ART. 2. Privateers shall not be admitted to the ports or roadsteads of the colony, except in the cases of accidents at sea, dangers of the sea, or want of provisions. They must depart immediately, as soon as the reasons for their admission have ceased to exist. They will not be allowed to take on board more provisions than are required to enable them to reach the nearest port of the country to which they belong, or that of one of its allies in the war, nor more coal than is needed for their consumption for twenty-four hours, at a maximum speed of 10 English miles per hour. They shall not be supplied with coal again within three months.

ART. 3. The vessels of war or privateers of the belligerents are not permitted to enter the ports or roadsteads of the colony with prizes, except in the case of accidents of the sea or want of provisions. As soon as the reasons for their admission have ceased to exist, they must depart immediately. They will not be permitted to take on board more provisions than they require in order to reach the nearest port of the country to which they belong, or that of one of its allies in the war. They shall not be supplied with coal so long as they are in possession of prizes. If vessels of war chased by the enemy take refuge in the territory of the colony, their prizes must be released.

ART. 4. The sale, exchange, or giving away of prizes or of articles taken therefrom, as also of captured goods, is prohibited in the ports, the roadsteads, and the territorial waters of the colony.

ART. 5. Ships and vessels of war, admitted in accordance with articles 1, 2, and 3, must not remain in the ports or roadsteads of the colony longer than therein provided. If, however, ships or vessels of war or others belonging to the belligerents should happen to be in the same port or roadstead of the colony, an interval of at least twenty-four hours must elapse between the departure of a ship or ships, or of a vessel or vessels, of one of the belligerents, and the subsequent departure of a ship or ships, or of a vessel or vessels, of the other. This interval may be lengthened according to circumstances.

ART. 6. The crews of ships or vessels of the belligerents must not come ashore armed—officers and under officers are excepted herefrom, as relates to the sword or hanger forming part of their uniform—and the boats must likewise not go about armed. If it should be desired, on the occasion of funeral ceremonies on shore, to be released from this prohibition, permission to that effect must be obtained from the governor.

BARGE, *Governor.*

WILLEMSTAD, *June 17, 1898.*

ECUADOR.

The following note has been received from the legation of Ecuador, dated New York, June 24, 1898:

Mr. SECRETARY: Having brought to the knowledge of my Government the contents of the various communications which your Department has addressed to me relative to the state of war which exists between the United States of America and the Kingdom of Spain, I have received instructions to state to you that the Government of Ecuador, while deploring the armed contest between two powers with which it maintains relations of good friendship and commerce, declares its absolute neutrality in accordance with the law of nations.

I avail, etc.,

L. F. CARBO.

Hon. W. R. DAY,
Secretary of State.

FRANCE.

The Department has received from Ambassador Porter, under date of Paris, April 27, 1898, translation of the declaration of neutrality of the French Government, as follows:

[Journal Officiel, April 27, 1898.]

The Government of the Republic declares and notifies whomsoever it may concern that it has decided to observe a strict neutrality in the war which has just broken out between Spain and the United States.

It considers it to be its duty to remind Frenchmen residing in France, in the colonies and protectorates, and abroad, that they must refrain from all acts which, committed in violation of French or international law, could be considered as hostile to one of the parties, or as contrary to a scrupulous neutrality. They are particularly forbidden to enroll themselves or to take service either in the army on land or on board the ships of war of one or the other of the belligerents, or to contribute to the equipment or armament of a ship of war.

The Government decides in addition that no ship of war of either belligerent will be permitted to enter and to remain with her prizes in the harbors and anchorages of France, its colonies and protectorates, for more than twenty-four hours, except in the case of forced delay or justifiable necessity.

No sale of objects gained from prizes shall take place in the said harbors and anchorages.

Any person disobeying the above restrictions can have no claim to the protection of the Government or its agents, against the acts or measures which the belligerents might exercise or decree in accordance with the rules of international law, and such persons will be prosecuted, should there be cause, according to the laws of the Republic.

Consul Tourgée writes from Bordeaux, May 19, 1898:

Having been informed by the consul at Rotterdam that the Government of the Netherlands had refused to clear the Norwegian steamer *Fram* for a Spanish port with a cargo of refined saltpeter, and that the same had accordingly cleared for Bayonne, France, a port in this consular district, I directed the consular agent at Pau to lodge a protest with the prefect of the department of Basses Pyrenees against said steamer being allowed to clear for any Spanish port. I also lodged a like protest with the superintendent of the marine of this district.

In response to this protest, the prefect of the Basses Pyrenees replies to-day (translated) as follows:

> I have the honor to inform you that the Minister of Foreign Affairs of the Republic of France, having been consulted by me by telegraph concerning the question of the detention of the *Fram*, advises me as follows:
>
> "Neutral governments are formally prohibited from furnishing, themselves, directly, munitions of war to belligerents; but the neutral state is not required to prevent the sending of arms and munitions by its subjects, and, for a much stronger reason, by strangers. Under these conditions, it is not incumbent on us to prevent the departure of the *Fram*, which you will allow to continue her voyage at her own risk and peril."

Thinking it may be a matter of interest to the Department to know exactly what are the instructions given to French officials in regard to the enforcement of its neutrality, I report the same direct.

GERMANY.

Ambassador White wrote from Berlin, under date of May 6, 1898, that in a speech delivered that day before the Reichstag, the Emperor said he considered it the task of his Government to observe strict neutrality in the war which had broken out between the United States and Spain.

In a communication dated May 5, Mr. White informed the Department that the German Secretary for Foreign Affairs stated that no public declaration of neutrality had been made by Germany, for the reason that it had been the policy of the Government, for the last twenty years, to abstain from such proclamations.

GIBRALTAR.

The proclamation of Gibraltar, expressed in the same terms as the proclamation of Great Britain,* was transmitted by Consul Sprague, of Gibraltar, under date of May 3, 1898.

---

*See p. 31.

GREAT BRITAIN.

Ambassador Hay writes from London, April 26, 1898:

I inclose two copies of the London Gazette Extraordinary of this date containing Her Britannic Majesty's proclamation of neutrality in relation to the war between the United States and Spain.

The inclosure reads:

THE LONDON GAZETTE EXTRAORDINARY.—PUBLISHED BY AUTHORITY.

Tuesday, April 26, 1898.

BY THE QUEEN.—A PROCLAMATION.

VICTORIA, R.

Whereas we are happily at peace with all sovereigns, powers, and states; and

Whereas a state of war unhappily exists between His Majesty the King of Spain, and, in his name and during his minority, Her Majesty the Queen Regent of the Kingdom, and the United States of America, and between their respective subjects, citizens, and others inhabiting within their countries, territories, or dominions; and

Whereas we are on terms of friendship and amicable intercourse with each of these powers, and with their several subjects, citizens, and others inhabiting within their countries, territories, or dominions; and

Whereas great numbers of our loyal subjects reside and carry on commerce, and possess property and establishments, and enjoy various rights and privileges within the dominions of each of the aforesaid powers, protected by the faith of treaties between us and each of the aforesaid powers; and

Whereas we, being desirous of preserving to our subjects the blessings of peace, which they now happily enjoy, are firmly purposed and determined to maintain a strict and impartial neutrality in the said state of war unhappily existing between the aforesaid powers; and

Whereas we are resolved to insure, by every lawful means in our power, the due observance by our subjects towards both the aforesaid powers of the rules embodied in Article VI of the treaty of the 8th of May, 1871, between us and the United States of America, which said rules are as follows:—

"A neutral government is bound—

"First. To use due diligence to prevent the fitting out, arming, or equipping, within its jurisdiction, of any vessel which it has reasonable ground to believe is intended to cruise or to carry on war against a power with which it is at peace; and also to use like diligence to prevent the departure from its jurisdiction of any vessel intended to cruise or carry on war as above, such vessel having been specially adapted, in whole or in part, within such jurisdiction, to warlike use.

"Secondly. Not to permit or suffer either belligerent to make use of its ports or waters as the base of naval operations against the other, or for the purpose of the renewal or augmentation of military supplies or arms, or the recruitment of men.

"Thirdly. To exercise due diligence in its own ports and waters, and, as to all persons within its jurisdiction, to prevent any violation of the foregoing obligations and duties."

We, therefore, have thought fit, by and with the advice of our Privy Council, to issue this our royal proclamation:

And we do hereby strictly charge and command all our loving subjects to govern themselves accordingly, and to observe a strict neutrality in and during the aforesaid war, and to abstain from violating or contravening either the laws and statutes of the Realm in this behalf, or the law of nations in relation thereto, as they will answer to the contrary at their peril:

And whereas in and by a certain statute made and passed in a session of Parliament holden in the thirty-third and thirty-fourth year of our reign, intituled "An act to regulate the conduct of Her Majesty's subjects during the existence of hostilities between foreign states with which Her Majesty is at peace," it is, amongst other things, declared and enacted as follows.

This act shall extend to all the dominions of Her Majesty, including the adjacent territorial waters:

"*Illegal enlistment.*"

"If any person, without the license of Her Majesty, being a British subject, within or without Her Majesty's dominions, accepts or agrees to accept any commission or engagement in the military or naval service of any foreign state at war with any foreign state at peace with Her Majesty, and in this act referred to as a friendly state, or whether a British subject or not, within Her Majesty's dominions, induces any other person to accept or agree to accept any commission or engagement in the military or naval service of any such foreign state as aforesaid,—

"He shall be guilty of an offense against this act, and shall be punishable by fine and imprisonment, or either of such punishments, at the discretion of the court before which the offender is convicted; and imprisonment, if awarded, may be either with or without hard labor.

"If any person without the license of Her Majesty, being a British subject, quits or goes on board any ship with a view of quitting Her Majesty's dominions, with intent to accept any commission or engagement in the military or naval service of any foreign state at war with a friendly state, or, whether a British subject or not, within Her Majesty's dominions, induces any other person to quit or go on board any ship with a view of quitting Her Majesty's dominions with a like intent,—

"He shall be guilty of an offense against this act, and shall be punishable by fine and imprisonment, or either of such punishments, at the discretion of the court before which the offender is convicted; and imprisonment, if awarded, may be either with or without hard labor.

"If any person induces any other person to quit Her Majesty's dominions or to embark on any ship within Her Majesty's dominions under a misrepresentation or false representation of the service in which such person is to be engaged, with the intent or in order that such person may accept or agree to accept any commission or engagement in the military or naval service of any foreign state at war with a friendly state,—

"He shall be guilty of an offense against this act, and shall be punishable by fine and imprisonment, or either of such punishments, at the discretion of the court before which the offender is convicted; and imprisonment, if awarded, may be either with or without hard labor.

"If the master or owner of any ship, without the license of Her Majesty, knowingly either takes on board or engages to take on board, or has on board such ship within Her Majesty's dominions any of the following persons, in this act referred to as illegally enlisted persons, that is to say:—

"(1) Any person who, being a British subject within or without the dominions of Her Majesty, has, without the license of Her Majesty, accepted or agreed to accept any commission or engagement in the military or naval service of any foreign state at war with any friendly state:

"(2) Any person, being a British subject, who, without the license of Her Majesty, is about to quit Her Majesty's dominions with intent to accept any commission or engagement in the military or naval service of any foreign state at war with a friendly state:

"(3) Any person who has been induced to embark under a misrepresentation or false representation of the service in which such person is to be engaged, with the intent or in order that such person may accept or agree to accept any commission or engagement in the military or naval service of any foreign state at war with a friendly state:

"Such master or owner shall be guilty of an offense against this act, and the following consequences shall ensue; that is to say,—

"(1) The offender shall be punishable by fine and imprisonment, or either of such punishments, at the discretion of the court before which the offender is convicted; and imprisonment, if awarded, may be either with or without hard labor: and

"(2) Such ship shall be detained until the trial and conviction or acquittal of the master or owner, and until all penalties inflicted on the master or owner have been paid, or the master or owner has given security for the payment of such penalties to the satisfaction of two justices of the peace, or other magistrate or magistrates having the authority of two justices of the peace: and

"(3) All illegally enlisted persons shall immediately on the discovery of the offense be taken on shore, and shall not be allowed to return to the ship.

"*Illegal shipbuilding and illegal expeditions.*

"If any person within Her Majesty's dominions, without the license of Her Majesty, does any of the following acts; that is to say:—

"(1) Builds or agrees to build, or causes to be built any ship with intent or knowledge, or having reasonable cause to believe that the same shall or will be employed in the military or naval service of any foreign state at war with any friendly state: or

"(2) Issues or delivers any commission for any ship with intent or knowledge, or having reasonable cause to believe that the same shall or will be employed in the military or naval service of any foreign state at war with any friendly state; or

"(3) Equips any ship with intent or knowledge, or having reasonable cause to believe that the same shall or will be employed in the military or naval service of any foreign state at war with any friendly state; or

"(4) Dispatches, or causes or allows to be dispatched, any ship with intent or knowledge, or having reasonable cause to believe that the same shall or will be employed in the military or naval service of any foreign state at war with any friendly state:

"Such person shall be deemed to have committed an offense against this act, and the following consequences shall ensue:

"(1) The offender shall be punishable by fine and imprisonment, or either of such punishments, at the discretion of the court before which the offender is convicted; and imprisonment, if awarded, may be either with or without hard labor.

"(2) The ship in respect of which any such offense is committed, and her equipment, shall be forfeited to Her Majesty.

"Provided that a person building, causing to be built, or equipping a ship in any of the cases aforesaid, in pursuance of a contract made before the commencement of such war as aforesaid, shall not be liable to any of the penalties imposed by this section in respect of such building or equipping if he satisfies the conditions following (that is to say):—

"(1) If forthwith upon a proclamation of neutrality being issued by Her Majesty he gives notice to the Secretary of State that he is so building, causing to be built, or equipping such ship, and furnishes such particulars of the contract and of any matters relating to, or done, or to be done under the contract as may be required by the Secretary of State:

"(2) If he gives such security, and takes and permits to be taken such other measures, if any, as the Secretary of State may prescribe for insuring that such ship shall not be dispatched, delivered, or removed without the license of Her Majesty until the termination of such war as aforesaid.

"Where any ship is built by order of or on behalf of any foreign state when at war with a friendly state, or is delivered to or to the order of such foreign state, or any person who to the knowledge of the person building is an agent of such foreign state, or is paid for by such foreign state or such agent, and is employed in the military or naval service of such foreign state, such ship shall, until the contrary is proved, be deemed to have been built with a view to being so employed, and the burden shall lie on the builder of such ship of proving that he did not know that the ship was intended to be so employed in the military or naval service of such foreign state.

"If any person within the dominions of Her Majesty, and without the license of Her Majesty,—

"By adding to the number of the guns, or by changing those on board for other guns, or by the addition of any equipment for war, increases or augments, or procures to be increased or augmented, or is knowingly concerned in increasing or augmenting the warlike force of any ship which at the time of her being within the dominions of Her Majesty was a ship in the military or naval service of any foreign state at war with any friendly state,—

"Such person shall be guilty of an offense against this act, and shall be punishable by fine and imprisonment, or either of such punishments, at the discretion of the court before which the offender is convicted; and imprisonment, if awarded, may be either with or without hard labor.

"If any person within the limits of Her Majesty's dominions, and without the license of Her Majesty:—

"Prepares or fits out any naval or military expedition to proceed against the dominions of any friendly state, the following consequences shall ensue:

"(1) Every person engaged in such preparation or fitting out, or assisting therein, or employed in any capacity in such expedition, shall be guilty of an offense against this act, and shall be punishable by fine and imprisonment, or either of such punishments, at the discretion of the court before which the offender is convicted; and imprisonment, if awarded, may be either with or without hard labor.

"(2) All ships, and their equipments, and all arms and munitions of war, used in or forming part of such expedition, shall be forfeited to Her Majesty.

"Any person who aids, abets, counsels, or procures the commission of any offense against this act shall be liable to be tried and punished as a principal offender."

And whereas by the said act it is further provided that ships built, commissioned, equipped, or dispatched in contravention of the said act, may be condemned and forfeited by judgment of the court of admiralty; and that if the Secretary of State or chief executive authority is satisfied that there is a reasonable and probable cause for believing that a ship within our dominions has been or is being built, commissioned, or equipped, contrary to the said act, and is about to be taken beyond the limits of such dominions, or that a ship is about to be dispatched contrary to the act, such Secretary of State, or chief executive authority, shall have power to issue a warrant authorizing the seizure and search of such ship and her detention until she has been either condemned or released by process of law. And whereas certain powers of seizure and detention are conferred by the said act on certain local authorities;

Now, in order that none of our subjects may unwarily render themselves liable to the penalties imposed by the said statute, we do hereby strictly command that no person or persons whatsoever do commit any act, matter, or thing whatsoever contrary to the provisions of the said statute, upon pain of the several penalties by the said statute imposed and of our high displeasure.

And we do hereby further warn and admonish all our loving subjects, and all persons whatsoever entitled to our protection, to observe towards each of the aforesaid powers, their subjects, citizens, and territories, and towards all belligerents whatsoever with whom we are at peace, the duties of neutrality; and to respect, in all and each of them, the exercise of belligerent rights.

And we hereby further warn all our loving subjects, and all persons whatsoever entitled to our protection, that if any of them shall presume, in contempt of this our royal proclamation, and of our high displeasure, to do any acts in derogation of their duty as subjects of a neutral power in a war between other powers, or in violation or contravention of the law of nations in that behalf, as more especially by breaking, or endeavoring to break, any blockade lawfully and actually established by or on behalf of either of the said powers, or by carrying officers, soldiers, dispatches, arms, ammunition, military stores or materials, or any article or articles considered and deemed to be contraband of war according to the law or modern usages of nations, for the use or service of either of the said powers that all persons so offending, together with their ships and goods, will rightfully incur and be justly liable to hostile capture, and to the penalties denounced by the law of nations in that behalf.

And we do hereby give notice that all our subjects and persons entitled to our protection who may misconduct themselves in the premises will do so at their peril, and of their own wrong; and that they will in nowise obtain any protection from us against such capture or such penalties as aforesaid, but will, on the contrary, incur our high displeasure by such misconduct.

Given at our court at St. James's, this 23d day of April, in the year of our Lord 1898, in the sixty-first year of our reign.

God save the Queen.

---

*The Right Honorable Sir Matthew White Ridley, Bart., M. P., to the Lords Commissioners of the Admiralty.**

FOREIGN OFFICE, *April 23, 1898.*

MY LORDS: Her Majesty being fully determined to observe the duties of neutrality during the existing state of war between Spain and the United States of America; being, moreover, resolved to prevent, as far as possible, the use of Her Majesty's harbors, ports, and coasts, and the waters within Her Majesty's territorial jurisdiction, in aid of the warlike purposes of either belligerent, and to insure, by every lawful means in Her power, the due observance by Her subjects towards both belligerent powers of the rules embodied in Article VI of the treaty of Washington of May 8, 1871, copies of which are herewith inclosed, has commanded me to

---

*Similar letters have been addressed to the Treasury, Home Office, Colonial Office, War Office, India Office, Scottish Office, and Board of Trade.

communicate to your Lordships, for your guidance, the following rules, which are to be treated and enforced as Her Majesty's orders and directions:

Rule 1.—During the continuance of the present state of war, all ships of war of either belligerent are prohibited from making use of any port or roadstead in the United Kingdom, the Isle of Man, or the Channel Islands, or in any of Her Majesty's colonies or foreign possessions or dependencies, or of any waters subject to the territorial jurisdiction of the British Crown, as a station or place of resort for any warlike purpose, or for the purpose of obtaining any facilities for warlike equipment; and no ship of war of either belligerent shall hereafter be permitted to leave any such port, roadstead, or waters from which any vessel of the other belligerent (whether the same shall be a ship of war or a merchant ship) shall have previously departed until after the expiration of at least twenty-four hours from the departure of such last-mentioned vessel beyond the territorial jurisdiction of Her Majesty.

Rule 2.—If there is now in any such port, roadstead, or waters subject to the territorial jurisdiction of the British Crown any ship of war of either belligerent, such ship of war shall leave such port, roadstead, or waters, within such time not less than twenty-four hours as shall be reasonable, having regard to all the circumstances and the condition of such ship as to repairs, provisions, or things necessary for the subsistence of her crew; and if after the date hereof any ship of war of either belligerent shall enter any such port, roadstead, or waters, subject to the territorial jurisdiction of the British Crown, such ship shall depart and put to sea within twenty-four hours after her entrance into any such port, roadstead, or waters, except in case of tress of weather, or of her requiring provisions or things necessary for the subsistence of her crew, or repairs; in either of which cases the authorities of the port, or of the nearest port (as the case may be), shall require her to put to sea as soon as possible after the expiration of such period of twenty-four hours, without permitting her to take in supplies beyond what may be necessary for her immediate use; and no such vessel which may have been allowed to remain within British waters for the purpose of repair shall continue in any such port, roadstead, or waters for a longer period than twenty-four hours after her necessary repairs shall have been completed. Provided, nevertheless, that in all cases in which there shall be any vessels (whether ships of war or merchant ships) of both the said belligerent parties in the same port, roadstead, or waters within the territorial jurisdiction of Her Majesty, there shall be an interval of not less than twenty-four hours between the departure therefrom of any such vessel (whether a ship of war or merchant ship) of the one belligerent and the subsequent departure therefrom of any ship of war of the other belligerent; and the time hereby limited for the departure of such ships of war respectively shall always, in case of necessity, be extended so far as may be requisite for giving effect to this proviso, but no further or otherwise.

Rule 3.—No ship of war of either belligerent shall hereafter be permitted, while in any such port, roadstead, or waters subject to the territorial jurisdiction of Her Majesty, to take in any supplies, except provisions and such other things as may be requisite for the subsistence of her crew, and except so much coal only as may be sufficient to carry such vessel to the nearest port of her own country, or to some nearer destination, and no coal shall again be supplied to any such ship of war in the same or any other port, roadstead, or waters subject to the territorial jurisdiction of Her Majesty, without special permission, until after the expiration of three months from the time when such coal may have been last supplied to her within British waters as aforesaid.

Rule 4.—Armed ships of either belligerent are interdicted from carrying prizes made by them into the ports, harbors, roadsteads, or waters of the United Kingdom, the Isle of Man, the Channel Islands, or any of Her Majesty's colonies or possessions abroad.

The governor or other chief authority of each of Her Majesty's territories or possessions beyond the seas shall forthwith notify and publish the above rules.

I have, etc.,

M. W. RIDLEY.

(Inclosure.)

Rules annexed to Article VI of the treaty between Her Majesty and the United States of America, signed at Washington May 8, 1871.

A neutral government is bound—

First. To use due diligence to prevent the fitting out, arming, or equipping, within its jurisdiction, of any vessel which it has reasonable ground to believe is intended to cruise or to carry on war against a power with which it is at peace; and also to use like diligence to prevent the departure from its jurisdiction of any vessel intended to cruise or carry on war as above, such vessel having been specially adapted, in whole or in part, within such jurisdiction, to warlike use.

Secondly. Not to permit or suffer either belligerent to make use of its ports or waters as the base of naval operations against the other, or for the purpose of the renewal or augmentation of military supplies of arms, or the recruitment of men.

Thirdly. To exercise due diligence in its own ports and waters, and, as to all persons within its jurisdiction, to prevent any violation of the foregoing obligations and duties.

GREECE.

Under date of May 5, 1898, Minister Rockhill sends from Belgrade translation of a note from the Minister of Foreign Affairs of Greece, as follows:

ATHENS, *April 16-28, 1898.*

Mr. MINISTER: I had the honor to receive the telegram which you were pleased to send me from Constantinople the 14th-26th instant to inform me that the Congress of the United States of America, by an act approved the 13th-25th of April, had declared that a state of war exists with Spain since the 9th-21st of April, inclusively.

In the name of the Royal Government, I take note of this declaration, and I have the honor to inform you that the strictest neutrality will be observed by Greece during the war which has broken out between the United States of America and Spain.

Please accept, etc.,

ALEXANDRE ZAIINIS.

The proclamation of neutrality by Greece, sent by Minister Rockhill under date of May 30, reads:

Greece maintaining friendly relations with the United States of America and Spain, the Greek Government will observe during the war between the two countries complete and strict neutrality, according to the laws of this country and international law. This has been declared to the Government of the United States, which had announced to this Government that the United States were now in a state of war with Spain.

GUATEMALA.

Under date of Guatemala, April 28, 1898, Mr. Hunter, United States minister to Guatemala and Honduras, transmits to the Department the following note from the Minister of Foreign Relations of Guatemala:

NATIONAL PALACE,
OFFICE OF THE SECRETARY OF FOREIGN RELATIONS,
REPUBLIC OF GUATEMALA,
Guatemala, April 27, 1898.

Mr. MINISTER: I have the honor to acknowledge the receipt of Your Excellency's attentive note of yesterday, in which you are pleased to communicate to me a dispatch from the Honorable John Sherman, Secretary of State, announcing that from the 21st instant there exists a state of war between the United States and Spain, and consequently desiring to know the attitude of the Government of Guatemala in the struggle.

In answer, I have the honor to inform Your Excellency, in order that through your worthy medium it may become known to the Cabinet at Washington, that the Government of Guatemala will faithfully comply with the laws of neutrality as prescribed by the universally accepted principles of international law.

I take advantage of this opportunity to renew to Your Excellency the assurance of my most distinguished consideration.

F. ANGUIANO.

His Excellency W. GODFREY HUNTER,
  Envoy Extraordinary and Minister Plenipotentiary of the United States.

HAITI.

Minister Powell sends from Port au Prince, under date of April 27, 1898, the following copy of the proclamation of neutrality:

A conflict regrettable in all points has just armed one against the other the two Governments of Spain and of the United States of America, to which the Government of the Republic of Haiti is bound by friendly relations that it desires to maintain and conserve, in observing the most strict neutrality between the belligerents.

The Government recognizes its obligations and will conform to the principles that govern them.

Further, while its general duties, based on the law of nations, will be strictly observed, the conventional duties by which it finds itself bound toward one of the belligerents, and which a public treaty has fixed at a far remote period, will be equally observed.

Nevertheless, if the treaty of friendship, of commerce, of navigation, and of extradition with the United States, in force since 1864, at an epoch when the war could not have been foreseen, places the Government of the Republic under obligation to follow a certain line of conduct (fixed beforehand by articles 30 and 31), the principles from which the treaty has not derogated, relative to refuge and asylum of vessels of war in national ports, to wrecks of merchant vessels on the coast and in the ports of the country, to maritime commerce, and to contraband of war, will be equitably put into practice in favor of both of the belligerents.

But the Republic makes a pressing appeal to the Governments of the United States and of Spain not to lose sight of the obligations toward neutrals that the law of nations imposes on belligerents.

The instructions sent by the Government to the several ports of the Republic were transmitted by Mr. Powell under date of May 18:

[Translation.]

PORT AU PRINCE, *May 9, 1898.*

To the SECRETARY OF WAR AND THE NAVY.

MY DEAR COLLEAGUE: The Government of the Republic, desiring to observe the strictest neutrality during the war which has just broken out between the United States of America and Spain, I communicate to you, as it has been decided, the following notes to serve as the basis for the instructions that the Government is to forward to the military commandants, including the delegates of the Government, to the chiefs of the ports, and to officials of the Government.

Our citizens, as well as the foreign residents of whatsoever nationality, should abstain from all acts that may invite reprisals. Popular manifestations in public places or in the streets; the raising of any emblems that may be considered offensive to one of the parties; the establishment of recruiting offices, secret or public, for natives or for foreigners; the embarkation on board of vessels of war in the service of the belligerents in passage in our ports, harbors, etc. (with the exception of pilots, whose services may be required at the entrance of the ports by one or the other party)—should be interdicted on all points of the territory.

Rigor must not, however, be pushed so far as to prevent the departure of the foreign residents on board of merchant vessels of neutral powers, for this might justly produce another but none the less regrettable source of conflict.

It shall be especially forbidden to foreign vessels to arm themselves as privateers, and to citizens to take part in supplying such equipment.

With confidence that reciprocity will be used in regard to the Haitian flag, the merchant vessels of the belligerents that enter our ports shall be authorized to take cargo and be cleared for foreign ports, on condition of not embarking either contraband of war or illicit merchandise of any kind.

It shall be equally prohibited to national vessels to carry articles called contraband of war, as well as regular troops or simple volunteers, for the account of one or the other of the belligerents.

It shall be permitted to vessels of war to take water, provisions, and coal in quantity necessary to reach the nearest port of their country.

If vessels of war in the service of the belligerents enter our ports, with or without prizes, these vessels may sail at any time, provided there be in the port no vessel of war of the other belligerent; and if by chance there should be one, a delay of twenty-four hours should intervene between the departure of the two vessels. The rule to be followed in the execution of this provision is: When two hostile vessels of war find themselves in the same port and desire to leave, international usage requires that preference be given to the vessel that arrived first. However, as this usage subjects the vessel last arrived to the ill will of its adversary, an expedient, both simple and just, has been adopted.

It consists in authorizing the last arrived to put to sea at its convenience, notifying the competent authorities twenty-four hours in advance, so that its adversary may, in case of need, take advantage of the preference that it has acquired, the delay then beginning only from the moment when the vessel is in condition to leave port.

On the other hand, international law and the treaty of 1864 require that vessels of war, during their sojourn in a port, should commit no act of violence towards hostile vessels. They can not augment the number and caliber of their guns, or purchase or embark arms and ammunition. They are forbidden to reinforce their crew or to accept voluntary recruits, even among their citizens. They should abstain from all inquiry concerning the forces, the positions, or the resources of the enemy. They can not employ either force or stratagem to regain prizes taken from their fellow-citizens, or to deliver prisoners of their country. They are prohibited to sell in our ports prizes they have brought in, or to leave them there, unless it is impossible for the captured to go to sea, in which case the question shall be immediately referred to the Government.

With the object of acting in concert with the military commandants and the chiefs of the ports in the execution of your instructions, the officials of the Government and their substitutes (and I have just written in this sense to my colleague of the Department of Justice) shall hold themselves always at the disposition of these officers. If the official of the Government is required by the military officers of ports that are not open, in case vessels in distress should present themselves, the official of the Government, or one of his substitutes, should immediately go to the residence of the officer; but should never cause the officers of the foreign vessel to be brought under an escort or otherwise, unless it be on their written request. In this case, they should be treated with all the respect due to their rank, and receive the necessary facilities for their voyage to an open port. The official shall immediately inform the Government, which shall take note thereof.

Wounded men, in case they are landed, should be treated with the respect due to their rank and with all humanity.

After their recovery, they can not again embark on board of a vessel of war of their nation, but they shall have the privilege of leaving the country on board of a merchant vessel belonging to a neutral nation.

In regard to prisoners that vessels of war in distress desire to land, the authorities shall permit the same, but on condition that, once on shore, they regain their liberty and have the option of leaving, when they desire, on board of merchant vessels of a neutral nation.

Permit me to insist on the following point, to wit, that the Government official and the substitute that he may delegate to replace him in his relations to the military officers or the chiefs of the ports shall act as advisers to the said officers, and shall always be present at the conferences, interviews, and audiences and take part in the discussions when their presence is necessary; they are, in a word, expected to see and foresee everything, so as to avoid conflicts.

In any and every case, the usage and customs of maritime etiquette shall be observed by our vessels of war toward those of the two belligerents, on the footing of the most perfect equality.

Our vessels shall also abstain from all acts of violence toward a belligerent vessel that shall violate the principles of international law, until it shall have received instructions from the Government.

The Secretary of State for Foreign Relations,

B. ST. VICTOR.

ITALY.

Ambassador Draper sends from Rome, under date of April 26, 1898, an extract from the Gazetta Ufficiale of April 25, which is translated as follows:

MINISTRY OF FOREIGN AFFAIRS.

I.

Proclamation of the neutrality of Italy in the war between Spain and the United States.

Spain and the United States of America finding themselves in a state of war, and Italy being in peace with both these powers, it behooves the Government of the King and the citizens of the Realm to scrupulously observe the obligations of neutrality, conformably to the laws in force and to the general principles of the laws of nations. If any Italian citizen shall violate these duties, he shall not be able to invoke the protection of the Royal Government or of its agents, and will incur moreover the penalty imposed by the special and general laws of the State.

II.

The ambassador of the United States in Rome, under note of date 23d instant, has communicated to the Royal Minister of Foreign Affairs the following two telegrams of the Department of State:

First. By proclamation under date of to-day (April 22) and following the resolutions of Congress approved the 20th, the President proclaims the blockade of the ports of the north coast of Cuba between Cardenas and Bahia Honda, as well as the blockade of Cienfuegos on the south coast.

Second. In case of hostilities between the United States and Spain, the Federal Government intends not to resort to privateering, but to adhere to the following rules recognized by international law:

(1) The neutral flag covers the enemy's goods, with the exception of contraband of war.

(2) Neutral goods, with the exception of contraband of war,* are not subject to seizure under enemy's flag.

(3) A blockade to be obligatory must be effective.

---

* In regard to contraband of war, Article XV of the treaty of commerce and navigation of the 26th of February, 1871, between Italy and the United States thus declares:

"The liberty of navigation and commerce secured to neutrals by the stipulations of this treaty shall extend to all kinds of merchandise, excepting those only which are distinguished by the name of contraband of war. And, in order to remove all causes of doubt and misunderstanding upon this subject, the contracting parties expressly agree and declare that the following articles and no others, shall be considered as comprehended under this denomination:

"(1) Cannons, mortars, howitzers, swivels, blunderbusses, muskets, guns, rifles, carbines, pistols, pikes, swords, sabers, lances, spears, halberds, bombs, grenades, powder, matches, balls, and all other things belonging to, and expressly manufactured for, the use of these arms.

"(2) Infantry belts, implements of war and defensive weapons, clothes cut or made up in a military form and for a military use.

"(3) Cavalry belts, war saddles, and holsters.

"(4) And generally, all kinds of arms and instruments of iron, steel, brass, and copper, or of any other materials, manufactured, prepared, and formed expressly to make war by sea or land."

Laws in regard to the enforcement of neutrality, including decrees of April 6, 1864, and June 16, 1895, in regard to the treatment of vessels of belligerents, and certain articles of the mercantile marine code were received from Mr. Draper under date of May 28:

DECREE OF APRIL 6, 1864.

ARTICLE I. No vessel of war or armed for cruising of any belligerent state shall be allowed to enter and remain with prizes in the ports or roadsteads of the Kingdom, except in the case of arrival under stress.

ART. II. In case of arrival under stress, the men-of-war or cruisers mentioned in the preceding article, and in the conditions there specified, must leave the coasts of the Kingdom immediately on cessation of the cause that obliged them to take refuge there, saving the provision of Article XI.

ART. III. No sale, exchange, barter, or gift of articles derived from the prizes shall take place under any pretext in the ports or roadsteads or on the coasts of the Kingdom.

ART. IV. Every Italian subject soever is forbidden to take commission from the belligerent parties to arm vessels for warfare, or to accept letters of marque for maritime cruising, or to assist in any way whatever in fitting out, arming, or preparing a vessel for warfare, or cruiser belonging to the belligerent parties above mentioned.

ART. V. In accordance with Article XXXV of the penal code for the mercantile marine, every subject of the Kingdom of Italy is forbidden to enroll himself or to take service in the ships of war or in those armed for cruising belonging to one of the belligerent states.

ART. VI. Those subjects who may contravene the provisions of the preceding Articles IV and V, or commit any act in regard to one of the belligerent powers contrary to the obligations of the neutrality maintained by the Italian Government toward the aforesaid parties, can not claim protection against the acts or measures whatever they may be which the belligerent parties may think fit to do or to take concerning them, without prejudice to the penalties which by the effects of Article V of the present decree are threatened to them, by the provision in Article LXXX of the penal code for the mercantile marine, dated January 13, 1827.

ART. VII. No belligerent ship of war or cruiser can remain more than twenty-four hours in a port or roadstead, or on the coasts of the Kingdom, or in the adjacent waters, even when it comes there alone, except in case of arrival under stress on account of bad weather, of damages, or want of the necessary provisions for the safety of the voyage.

ART. VIII. Ships of war belonging to a friendly power, even though belligerent, may come to and remain in the ports or roadsteads or on the coasts of the Kingdom, provided that the purpose of their mission be exclusively scientific.

ART. IX. In no case can a belligerent ship make use of an Italian port for purpose of warfare or to supply itself with arms or ammunition. It can not, under pretext of repairs, execute works in any way adapted to increase its warlike force.

ART. X. Nothing shall be supplied to belligerent ships of war or cruisers excepting provisions, commodities, and things for repairs, simply necessary for the subsistence of their crews and the safety of their voyage. Such belligerent ships of war or cruisers as wish to resupply themselves with coal shall not receive that supply until twenty-four hours after their arrival.

ART. XI. If ships of war, cruisers, or merchant vessels belonging to the two belligerent parties should be at the same time in a port or roadstead or on the coast of the Kingdom, there must be an interval of at least twenty-four hours between the departure of any vessel of one belligerent party and that following of any ship of the other party. This interval may be increased according to the circumstances by the maritime authority of the place.

ART. XIV.* The maritime authorities of the places specified in the preceding article,† on the arrival of foreign ships of war, are to transmit to the commanders or commanders in chief thereof a copy of the present regulations for their guidance, with an invitation to observe them.

ART. XV. The maritime authorities of the Kingdom are to see to the exact fulfillment of the enactments of the present decree, which is to take effect from the day of its publication in the various ports of the Kingdom.

ART. XVI. All the enactments now in force are abrogated in such part as may be contrary to the present decree.

ARTICLES OF THE MERCANTILE MARINE CODE REGARDING THE NEUTRALITY OF PORTS AND THE PENALTIES FOR CITIZENS WHO VIOLATE NEUTRALITY.

ART. 246. In case of war among powers toward which the State has neutral relations, privateers or men-of-war with prizes shall not be allowed to enter ports, roadsteads, or harbors of the State, except in case of arrival under stress. As soon as the danger is passed the ship must leave. No man-of-war or belligerent privateer will be permitted to remain more than twenty-four hours in any port, roadstead, or harbor of the State, or in the adjacent waters, even if it should present itself alone, except in case of stress of weather, or on account of injuries or lack of provisions necessary to safe navigation. In no case will the sale, exchange, barter, or gift of prizes be permitted in the ports, roadsteads, or harbors of the State.

ART. 247. War ships of a friendly power, even when belligerent, can enter or remain in the ports, roadsteads, or harbors of the State, provided the object of their mission be exclusively scientific.

ART. 248. In no case can a belligerent ship make use of an Italian port for war purposes or to provision itself with arms or munitions. No work can be executed under pretext of repairs which in any way could add to the fighting strength of the vessel.

ART. 249. To men-of-war or privateers of belligerents there will be furnished only food and provisions and means of repairs actually necessary to the sustenance of their crews and to the safety of their navigation. Men-of-war or privateers of belligerents wishing to recoal can not obtain this supply until after a delay of twenty-four hours from the time of their arrival.

ART. 250. When men-of-war, privateers, or mercantile vessels of the two belligerent parties meet in a port, roadstead, or harbor of the State, an interval of at least twenty-four hours must intervene between the departure of any boat of one belligerent and that of any boat of the other. This interval can be increased, according to circumstances, by the maritime authority of the place.

ART. 251. The taking of prizes or any act of hostility committed by ships of the belligerent nations in the territorial sea or in the waters adjacent to the State shall constitute a violation of territory.

ART. 380. The captain or master who shall assume command of a foreign war

---

* Articles XII and XIII of the present decree were abrogated by article 16 of the royal decree of June 16, 1895.

† The abrogated Article XIII of the present decree enumerated the sea fortresses of that time. The following were substituted by article 8 of the royal decree of April 21, 1895:

ART. 8. The following localities are sea fortresses: Vado, Savona, Genoa, Spezia, Monte Argentario, (Talamone), Port St. Stephen, Gaeta, La Maddelena, and the adjacent islands and coast of Sardinia, Messina, and the dependent anchorages, both sides of the Straits Tarentum, Ancona, Venice, and the anchorages in the lagoons.

ship without having obtained permission of the Government will be dismissed, without prejudice to the other penalties which he may incur from the fact of having taken military service with a foreign nation.

ART. 381. All persons inscribed on the sailors' rolls or registers who embark on mercantile vessels belonging to a power at war with the State incur the penalty of imprisonment of from three months to a year.

ART. 382. Italians who shall enlist on privateers or war ships of powers at war with the State will be punished by imprisonment with forced labor. Whenever they take part in acts of depredation against ships of their own country, they incur the penalties prescribed for those who take up arms against the State.

EXTRACT FROM THE ROYAL DECREE OF JUNE 16, 1895, WHICH GOVERNS IN TIME OF PEACE THE LANDING AND THE STAY OF FOREIGN MEN-OF-WAR IN PORTS AND ON COASTS OF THE KINGDOM.

ART. 11. War ships of hostile powers which are in territorial waters are forbidden to commit acts of hostility toward each other. In case of violation of this rule, those ships which do not obey a notice to desist are treated as enemies by national forts and men-of-war.

ART. 12. Foreign ships of war and merchantmen armed for cruising are forbidden to bring prizes into, or to arrest and search vessels in, the territorial sea or in the sea adjacent to the Italian islands, as well as to commit other acts which constitute an offense to the rights of state sovereignty.

ART. 15. In case of transgression, it is the duty of the local military marine authority, or, in his absence, of the chief officer of the port, and, in the absence of this official, of the military authority on land, to notify foreign ships of war of the strict observance of the regulations contained in the present decree. In case of persistence in transgression or of refusal to comply with the notice, the said authorities will formally protest and will immediately telegraph the information to the proper head of the department, or to the naval or military commandant, or to the Minister of War or of the Navy, according to the jurisdiction under which they may be placed.

JAMAICA.

Consul Dent sends from Jamaica, under date of April 26, a copy of the Jamaica Gazette Extraordinary, containing the following proclamation of the governor on the subject of neutrality:

THE JAMAICA GAZETTE EXTRAORDINARY.

Saturday, April 23, 1898.

GOVERNMENT NOTICE.

COLONIAL SECRETARY'S OFFICE, *April 23, 1898.*

His excellency has received intimation from the Secretary of State for the Colonies that a state of war unhappily exists between the Kingdom of Spain and the Republic of the United States of America.

His excellency therefore hereby strictly charges and commands British subjects and others in the colony to observe a strict and impartial neutrality in and during the aforesaid war and to abstain from violating or contravening the foreign enlistment act, and the rules following shall be in force and shall be strictly observed from this date:—

1. During the continuance of the present state of war, all ships of war of either

belligerent are prohibited from making use of any port or roadstead in the United Kingdom, the Isle of Man, or the Channel Islands, or in any of Her Majesty's colonies or foreign possessions or dependencies or of any waters subject to the territorial jurisdiction of the British Crown, as a station, or place of resort, for any warlike purpose, or for the purpose of obtaining any facilities for warlike equipment; and no ship of war of either belligerent shall hereafter be permitted to sail out of or leave any port, roadstead, or waters subject to British jurisdiction, from which any vessel of the other belligerent (whether the same shall be a ship of war or a merchant ship) shall have previously departed, until after the expiration of at least twenty-four hours from the departure of such last-mentioned vessel beyond the territorial jurisdiction of Her Majesty.

2. If any ship of war of either belligerent shall, after the time when this order shall be first notified and put in force in the United Kingdom, the Isle of Man, and the Channel Islands, and in the several colonies and foreign possessions or dependencies of Her Majesty, respectively, enter any port, roadstead, or waters belonging to Her Majesty, either in the United Kingdom, the Isle of Man, or the Channel Islands, or in any of Her Majesty's colonies or foreign possessions or dependencies, such vessel shall be required to depart and to put to sea within twenty-four hours after her entrance into such port, roadstead, or waters, except in case of stress of weather, or of her requiring provisions or things necessary for the subsistence of her crew, or repairs; in either of which cases the authorities of the port, or of the nearest port (as the case may be), shall require her to put to sea as soon as possible after the expiration of such period of twenty-four hours, without permitting her to take in supplies beyond what may be necessary for her immediate use, and no such vessel which may have been allowed to remain within British waters for the purpose of repair shall continue in any such port, roadstead, or waters, for a longer period than twenty-four hours after her necessary repairs shall have been completed. Provided, nevertheless, that in all cases in which there shall be any vessel (whether ships of war or merchant ships) of the said belligerent parties in the same port, roadstead, or waters within the territorial jurisdiction of Her Majesty, there shall be an interval of not less than twenty-four hours between the departure therefrom of any such vessel (whether a ship of war or merchant ship) of the one belligerent, and the subsequent departure therefrom of any ship of war of the other belligerent, and the time hereby limited for the departure of such ships of war resepectively shall always, in case of necessity, be extended so far as may be requisite for giving effect to this proviso, but no further or otherwise.

3. No ship of war of either belligerent shall hereafter be permitted, while in any port, roadstead, or waters subject to the territorial jurisdiction of Her Majesty, to take in any supplies, except provisions and such other things as may be requisite for the subsistence of her crew, and except so much coal only as may be sufficient to carry such vessel to the nearest port of her own country, or to some nearer destination, and no coal shall again be supplied to any such ship of war in the same or any other port, roadstead, or waters subject to the territorial jurisdiction of Her Majesty, without special permission, until after the expiration of three months from the time when such coal may have been last supplied to her within British waters as aforesaid.

4. Armed ships of either party are interdicted from carrying prizes made by them into the ports, harbors, roadsteads, or waters of the United Kingdom, the Isle of Man, the Channel Islands, or any of Her Majesty's colonies or possessions abroad.

By command. FRED. EVANS,
Colonial Secretary.

JAPAN.

Minister Buck incloses from Tokyo, under date of May 5, 1898, clippings from the Japan Times of May 3, being a translation of the imperial rescript and ordinances which composed the proclamation of neutrality officially announced on May 2. The inclosure reads:

IMPERIAL RESCRIPT.

War having unfortunately broken out between the United States of America and Spain, and being desirous of maintaining the amicable and friendly relations existing between this Empire and the belligerent powers, we hereby order the promulgation of regulations relating to neutrality. Our subjects and other persons resident within the dominions of the Empire shall, until the end of hostilities, observe the obligations of a strict neutrality in conformity with the general principles of international law and the provisions of the regulations herewith promulgated. Any person failing to observe these obligations, shall not only forfeit the protection of this Empire against the proceedings of one or the other of the belligerent powers, but also be liable to prosecution at the imperial courts of law in accordance with the provisions of the law.

[Imperial sign manual.]
[Privy seal.]

April 30, 1898.

(Countersigned,) Marquis HIROBUMI ITO,
Minister President of State.
Marquis TSUKUMICHI SAIGO,
Minister of the Navy.
Count KAORU INOUYE,
Minister of Finance.
Viscount AKIMASA YOSHIKAWA,
Minister of Home Affairs.
Baron TOKUJIRO NISHI,
Minister of Foreign Affairs.
Viscount TARO KATSURA,
Minister of War.
ARASUKE SONE,
Minister of Justice.
Baron KENCHO SUYEMATSU,
Minister of Communications.
KENTARO KANEKO,
Minister of Agriculture and Commerce.
KAZUMASU TOYAMA,
Minister of Education.

IMPERIAL ORDINANCE.

We hereby sanction the present ordinance relating to the conduct of our subjects and the foreigners resident within our dominions, during the continuance of hostilities between the United States of America and Spain, and order it to be promulgated.

[Imperial sign manual.]
[Privy seal.]

April 30, 1898.
    (Countersigned,)   Marquis HIROBUMI ITO,
        Minister President of State.
    Viscount AKIMASA YOSHIKAWA,
        Minister of Home Affairs.
    Baron TOKUJIRO NISHI,
        Minister of Foreign Affairs.
    ARASUKE SONE,
        Minister of Justice.

IMPERIAL ORDINANCE.—NO. LXXXVI.

In relation to the present war between the United States of America and Spain, the Japanese subjects and the citizens of foreign powers resident within the dominions of the Empire are not permitted to commit any of the acts specified below:

1. The obtaining from one or the other of the belligerent powers letters of marque or commission for capturing merchantmen by means of privateers.

2. The accepting service in the army or navy or engaging in any military operations of one or the other of the belligerent powers, enlisting as sailor, or accepting commission for service on board a vessel used for warlike purposes or privateers belonging to one or the other of the belligerent powers.

3. The making contracts with, or sending other individuals out of the dominions of the Empire, with the object of enabling the said individuals to enter upon the military or naval service of one or the other of the belligerent powers, or for the purpose of enabling them to enlist as sailors, or accept commissions to serve, on board ships used for warlike purposes or privateers.

4. The selling, purchasing, chartering, arming, or equipping ships with the object of supplying them to one or the other of the belligerent powers for use in war or privateering; the assisting such sale, purchase, chartering, arming, or equipping.

5. The supplying arms, ammunition, or other materials of direct use in fighting to the men-of-war, other ships used for warlike purposes, or privateers, belonging to one or the other of the belligerent powers. The present ordinance shall take effect from the day of its promulgation.

IMPERIAL ORDINANCE.

We hereby give our sanction to the present ordinance relating to the control of the war ships or other vessels connected with the warlike operations during the continuation of hostilities between the United States of America and Spain, and which are found in the territorial waters of the Empire, and order the same to be promulgated.

[Imperial sign manual.]
[Privy seal.]

April 30, 1898.
    (Countersigned,)   Marquis HIROBUMI ITO,
        Minister President of State.
    Marquis TSUKUMICHI SAIGO,
        Minister of the Navy.
    Viscount AKIMASA YOSHIKAWA,
        Minister of Home Affairs.
    Baron TOKUJIRO NISHI,
        Minister of Foreign Affairs.

IMPERIAL ORDINANCE.—NO. LXXXVII.

Such men-of-war and such other ships used for warlike purposes in connection with the present war between the United States of America and Spain as may happen to be in the territorial waters of the Empire shall be regulated in accordance with the rules mentioned below:

1. No privateer shall be allowed to come within the territorial waters of the Empire. In case, however, when it is compelled to enter such territorial waters on account of unavoidable circumstances, such as stress of weather, destitution of articles indispensable to navigation, or disablement, it should leave the territorial waters as soon as such circumstance shall have ceased to exist.

2. No man-of-war or other ship belonging to one or the other of the belligerent powers shall be permitted to commit any act of war, or visit, search, or capture merchantmen within the territorial waters of the Empire. Neither shall such man-of-war or such other ship be allowed to make use of any portion of the territorial waters of the Empire as the basis or headquarters of naval operations, or for any other warlike purposes whatever.

3. The men-of-war and other ships used for warlike purposes, belonging to one or the other of the belligerent powers, may enter any of the ports that are open to all ships for ordinary purposes of navigation, but should not stay in the waters of such port longer than twenty-four hours. In case when such men-of-war or such other ships used for warlike purposes have been compelled to seek the waters of such port on account of unavoidable circumstances, such as stress of weather, destitution of articles necessary for navigation, or disablement and are unable to quit the port within twenty-four hours, they should leave the territorial waters of the Empire as soon as such circumstance or circumstances shall have ceased to exist.

4. No man-of-war or other ships used for warlike purposes, belonging to one or the other of the belligerent powers, shall be permitted to take any captured vessel into the territorial waters of the Empire, except under stress of weather, or on account of destitution of articles necessary for navigation, or of disablement. In the last-mentioned case, it is not permissible under whatever pretext to land any prisoner of war or to dispose of the captured vessel or articles.

5. No man-of-war or other ship employed for warlike purposes belonging to one or the other of the belligerent powers shall be permitted either to recruit its crew or get supplies of arms, ammunition, or any other material of direct use in fighting within the dominions of the Empire. Neither shall such man-of-war or such other ships employed for purposes of warfare be permitted under whatever circumstances to receive repairs within the dominions of the Empire beyond what shall suffice to enable it to get back to the nearest port of its own country.

6. The men-of-war and other ships used for warlike purposes belonging to one or the other of the belligerent powers may get, in the ports of the Empire, supplies of articles necessary for their crews, also coal and other things indispensable to navigation, as well as of materials needed for repairs; but the quantity of such supplies should never exceed that which will be necessary for the purpose of taking such men-of-war and such other ships to the nearest port of their own country. Any of such men-of-war or such other ships which has once obtained a supply of coal shall not be permitted to get another supply until after the lapse of three full months.

7. When the men-of-war, or other ships used for warlike purposes, or privateers, of both belligerent powers happen to be simultaneously in the same port in the dominions of the Empire, the ships of one power shall not be allowed to leave the port until twenty-four hours shall have elapsed after the departure of those of the other power, unless under the directions of the Japanese naval commander in port or the chief local official. The present ordinance shall come in force from the day of its promulgation.

KOREA.

Minister Allen sends from Seoul, under date of April 28, 1898, the following copy of a note received from the Foreign Office:

> FOREIGN OFFICE,
> *Seoul, April 27, 1898.*

Chyo Pyengjik, Minister for Foreign Affairs, to the Hon. H. N. Allen, United States Minister.

SIR: I have the honor to acknowledge the receipt of Your Excellency's dispatch of to-day's date, concerning the state of war now existing between the United States and Spain.

In reply thereto, I have the honor to assure Your Excellency that my Government will observe the strictest neutrality in this affair.

I beg Your Excellency to convey this message to your Government.

I have, etc.

LEEWARD ISLANDS.

Under date of May 2, 1898, Consul Hunt, of Antigua, transmits copy of the Leeward Islands Gazette of April 23, containing a proclamation in the same terms (mutatis mutandis) as that of Great Britain,* except as to preamble.

LIBERIA.

Minister Smith sends from Monrovia, under date of June 24, copy of a proclamation of the President, as follows:

A PROCLAMATION BY THE PRESIDENT.

Whereas we are happily at peace with all nations, states, and powers; and

Whereas a state of war now exists between His Majesty the King of Spain, represented during his minority by Her Majesty the Queen Regent of the Kingdom, and the United States of America, and between their respective subjects and citizens; and

Whereas the Republic of Liberia is on terms of friendship and in treaty stipulations with each of these nations aforesaid; and

Whereas we are desirous of preserving these peaceful relations.

Therefore, it is our firm purpose and determination to maintain a strict neutrality in and during the said state of war now unhappily existing between the aforesaid nations.

We recognize as binding upon us as a state that system of national justice

---

*See p. 31.

known as the law of nations, as it is now generally accepted, and we do hereby enjoin all citizens of Liberia to abstain from committing any of the following acts:

(1) The fitting out, arming, or equipping or aiding in the same, within this jurisdiction of any vessel or vessels intended, or reasonably believed to be intended, to cruise or carry on war with or against either of the aforesaid belligerents.

(2) The supplying or aiding to furnish any guns, ammunitions, or other munitions of war.

(3) The illegal enlisting in the army or navy of either of the aforesaid belligerents.

All citizens of the Republic of Liberia are warned against committing any of the above acts or in any way contravening the laws of neutrality as above defined.

And our public officers (both civil, naval, and military) are hereby commanded and directed to exercise due diligence to see that our ports or waters are not used as a base of operations by either of the aforesaid belligerents against the other or for the purpose of repairing, renewal, or increase of military supplies or arms or vessels or enlisting of men.

Now, therefore, I, William David Coleman, by virtue of the authority vested in me as President of the Republic of Liberia, by and with the advice of the cabinet, do issue this proclamation.

And I strictly charge and command all citizens of Liberia, under the stern displeasure of the laws, to take notice and govern themselves accordingly in observing a strict and impartial neutrality in and during the state of war now waging and going on aforesaid, and to abstain from violating or contravening our Liberian statutes or the law of nations relating thereto.

Done at Monrovia, Liberia, on the 20th day of June, A. D. 1898, and the year of our independence the fifty-first.

W. D. COLEMAN,
President.

By the President:
G. W. GIBSON,
Secretary of State.

MALTA.

Consul Grout transmits from Malta, under date of April 25, 1898, a copy of the proclamation of neutrality as announced by the governor of Malta in the Official Gazette of the same date. The proclamation is in the same terms, mutatis mutandis, as that of Great Britain,* except as to preamble.

MAURITIUS.

Consul Campbell sends from Port Louis, under date of April 28, 1898, copy of the proclamation of neutrality by the colony of Mauritius, as published in the Planters' and Commercial Gazette, April 24-25, 1898. The proclamation is in the same terms, mutatis mutandis, as that of Great Britain.*

---

* See p. 31.

MEXICO.

Under date of April 30, 1898, Minister Clayton sends from Mexico, translation of a circular sent by the Secretary of the Interior to the governors of the various States of Mexico, enjoining strict neutrality; also translations of the circulars issued by the Secretary of the Treasury and by the Minister of Justice and Public Instruction, calling upon all persons connected with their respective departments to observe neutrality. The circulars read:

CIRCULAR OF SECRETARY OF THE INTERIOR TO THE GOVERNORS.

[From Diario Oficial, April 26, 1898.]

DEPARTMENT OF THE INTERIOR,
SECTION 2.—CIRCULAR No. 1233.

Judging from the latest cablegrams an outbreak of hostilities between the United States and Spain seems inevitable. The Government of Mexico, which during the events preceding the present situation has taken especial care to maintain for itself and the country the strictest neutrality, proposes now, more than ever, to change in no way its rule of conduct, and while it has the greatest confidence in the good sense of the Mexican people and in the discretion, aptitude, and patriotism of the several State governments, it believes, nevertheless, considering the gravity of the situation, in recommending to them as matter of the greatest importance, that efforts be redoubled so that in no way this strict neutrality may be violated. In this sense the President of the Republic has instructed me to address you, as well as the governors of the other States, to communicate the foregoing resolution, that it may be made known to the inhabitants, and especially to the officials and the employees under them, that the necessary steps may be taken to enforce compliance therewith; it being expected of your well-known high character that you will use your best efforts in seconding the elevated views of the Executive, repressing with firmness any contrary intent, with the object of avoiding, in official and private acts, any demonstration that is not in accordance with the attitude which Mexico must observe in the lamentable conflict between two friendly nations; also avoiding or suppressing, when not possible to so avoid, collisions between the sympathizers of the two contending countries.

Liberty and constitution.

MEXICO, *April 22, 1898.* GONZALES COSEO.

CIRCULAR ISSUED BY THE SECRETARY OF THE TREASURY.

[From Diario Oficial, April 27, 1898.]

DEPARTMENT OF THE TREASURY AND PUBLIC CREDIT,
THIRD SECTION.

In the deplorable conflict that has recently broken out between two nations friendly to Mexico, the Government of the Republic will observe, in compliance with its international duties, the strictest neutrality, and orders all public employees to conform to this order.

Therefore the President of the Republic has ordered that this Department make known this order to its employees, that they may scrupulously abstain from acts or manifestations departing from the reserved and impartial attitude which, in view of the said conflict, the people and Government of Mexico should observe.

The patrotism and discretion of the employees is relied upon to bring about exact compliance with the order which I communicate to you; but if, unfortunately, it be disobeyed, the corresponding administrative punishment will be inflicted without prejudice to whatever other punishment may be required in the case.

Kindly acknowledge the receipt.

MEXICO, *April 27, 1898.*
LIMANTOUR.

CIRCULAR OF MINISTER OF JUSTICE.

[From Diario Oficial, April 26, 1898.]

DEPARTMENT OF JUSTICE AND PUBLIC INSTRUCTION.

Under this date this Department has issued the following circular:

In the deplorable conflict that has recently begun between two nations friendly to Mexico, the Government of the Republic will observe, in compliance with its international duties, the strictest neutrality, and orders all public employees to conform to this order.

Therefore the President of the Republic has ordered that this Department make known this order to its employees, that they may scrupulously abstain from any acts or manifestations departing from the reserved and impartial attitude which, in view of the said conflict, the people and Government of Mexico should observe.

The patriotism and discretion of the employees is relied upon to effect an exact compliance with the order which I communicate to you; but if, unfortunately, it be disobeyed, the corresponding administrative penalty will be inflicted without preventing, in any way, other punishment that the case may require.

And by order of the President of the Republic I have the honor to notify the Supreme Court in order that it may be brought to the knowledge of the functionaries and employees of the judicial branch of the federation, and compliance with it recommended.

Liberty and constitution.

MEXICO, *April 27, 1898.*
J. BARANDA.

The circular of the Minister of War and Marine was sent by Minister Clayton under date of May 6:

[From Diario Oficial, April 31, 1898.]

DEPARTMENT OF WAR AND MARINE,
OFFICE OF GENERAL STAFF.—CIRCULAR NO. 209.

It being an international duty for the Government of the Mexican Republic to maintain the strictest neutrality in the war actually existing between the United States and Spain, its relations with both belligerents being equally friendly, it is the duty of all Mexican citizens, and especially of the members of the army, to be scrupulously alert, so that for no reason any violations of neutrality, however remote, may occur. In this sense, and at the express wish of the President, I recommend that you redouble your vigilance so that these prohibitions may be complied with by all generals, chiefs, officials, members of troops, and others subject to their orders.

The President believes that the patriotism and prudence of all the members of the army will be sufficient to sustain his designs; but if, unfortunately, anyone should forget his duty, he will be subject to the corresponding penalties without prejudice to those that may be inflicted under the military code for disobedience to this order.

I communicate this to you that it may be complied with, and that it may be published in the general order of the day in all the places where there are troops under your command.

Liberty and constitution.

MEXICO, *April 29, 1898.* BERRIOZABAL.

Under date of May 11, Mr. Clayton incloses the following:

[From Diario Oficial, May 7, 1898.]

DEPARTMENT OF WAR AND MARINE.

The President of the Republic has ordered, notwithstanding the express prohibition in the first instruction of the circular which I communicated to you privately on the 29th ultimo, inclosing the note of the Minister of Relations containing said instruction, that I especially charge you, as I now do, that for the purpose of establishing as a fact the strict neutrality of the Republic in the Spanish-American conflict, no vessel carrying provisions or money for either of the belligerent powers be, under any circumstances, dispatched, and that public reunions with the object of collecting means to assist either of the belligerent powers be prevented.

I communicate the same to you for your information and observance.

Liberty and constitution. A copy of the original.

MEXICO, *May 4, 1898.* ALEJANDRO PEZO.

NETHERLANDS.

Minister Newel sends from The Hague, under date of April 26, 1898, an announcement that neutrality will be observed by the Netherlands Government, which is translated as follows:

MINISTRY OF FOREIGN-AFFAIRS.

War having broken out between two powers friendly to the Netherlands, the Government of the Netherlands declares that it will observe the strictest neutrality towards the belligerents.

It reminds all citizens of the Netherlands, even those domiciled outside of Europe, that they must refrain from all acts that can be regarded as contrary to neutrality.

It directs their attention principally to acts prohibited by the rules of international law, that they may avoid participating in any way in the recruiting of soldiers, or in the fitting out of ships of war or privateers in the interest of the powers at war, and likewise to the danger connected with breaking an effective blockade, and with selling and furnishing munitions of war or other contraband goods to the belligerents, or conveying such articles to them. It further calls attention to the provisions of articles 100, 1°, 388, and 389, of the penal code, which are as follows:

"ART. 100, 1°. Any person who, in case of a war in which the Netherlands are not concerned, shall intentionally commit any act whereby the neutrality of the

State is endangered, or shall willfully violate any special provision for the maintenance of neutrality, adopted and proclaimed by the Government of the Netherlands, shall be punished by imprisonment for a term not exceeding six years.

"ART. 388. Any citizen of the Netherlands who shall accept letters of marque without the consent of the Government of the Netherlands, or shall engage in service as captain of a vessel which he knows to be intended for privateering without the permission of the Government of the Netherlands, shall be punished by imprisonment for a term not exceeding four years.

"ART. 389. Any citizen of the Netherlands who shall engage in service as a member of the crew on board of a vessel, knowing it to be intended for privateering, or to be used for that purpose, without the permission of the Government of the Netherlands, or who shall voluntarily remain in service after he shall have learned that the vessel is intended or used for privateering, shall be imprisoned for a term not exceeding three years."

The Government will tolerate no acts that can be considered as being in violation of the duties of a neutral state, and it warns all citizens of the Netherlands, wherever they may be domiciled, that they may rely upon its protection or its intervention in their behalf, only in case they carefully abstain from any violation of neutrality.

On May 3, 1898, Minister Newel sends the following orders respecting neutrality:

No. 1.

The Ministers of Foreign Affairs, Justice, Marine, and War, authorized thereto by Her Majesty the Queen Regent:

In observance of the royal order of February 2, 1893 (Official Gazette No. 46):

Hereby publicly notify all whom it may concern that, in observance of and with a view to the maintenance of perfect neutrality during the war which has broken out between two powers friendly to ourselves, namely, Spain on the one side and the United States of America on the other, the following regulations have been agreed upon:

ARTICLE I. It is forbidden to supply arms or ammunition to the ships of war or privateers of the powers at war, as also to render them any assistance whatever in the increasing of their crews, arming, or equipment, and in general to voluntarily perform any act that might endanger the neutrality of the State.

ART. II. It is moreover forbidden:

(*a*) To equip in this country ships of war or other vessels destined for any military end, in the interests of the parties at war, as also to convey or sell such like ships to the said parties;

(*b*) To export arms, ammunition, or other war material to the parties at war. Herein is included the exportation of everything that is adaptable for immediate use in war, but not those of unwrought materials, unless they can be immediately turned to warlike ends.

(*c*) To recruit military men within the territory of the State for the parties at war.

(*d*) To organize in any military way volunteers within the territory of the State, with the purpose of annexing them to the army of either of the parties at war.

The above-mentioned ministers further direct attention to articles 100, 388, and 389 of the penal code, and hereby caution all persons domiciled within the Kingdom against becoming involved in any way in privateering and against acceptance of any foreign privateering ships' papers, in view of the fact that all who shall carry on any privateering on such papers, or assist thereto, will be prosecuted before a Netherlands judicial authority.

Further, they direct the attention of ship commanders, shipping agents, and ships' freighters to the danger and detriment to which they would expose themselves by not respecting an actual blockade or by conveying for either of the parties at war contraband or military dispatches, in conflict with the obligations imposed upon neutral powers.

Persons rendering themselves guilty of such like actions are liable to whatever results may follow, without any protection or intervention whatever, or any claim thereto from Her Majesty's Government.

The above-mentioned ministers,

W. H. DE BEAUFORT.
CORT V. A. LINDEN.
RÖELL.
ELAND.

No. 2.

The Ministers for Foreign Affairs, Justice, Marine, and War, authorized thereto by Her Majesty the Queen Regent:

In observance of the royal order of February 2, 1893 (Official Gazette No. 46):

Hereby publicly notify all whom it may concern, that in observance of, and with a view to the maintenance of, perfect neutrality during the war which has broken out between two powers friendly to ourselves, namely, Spain on the one side and the United States of America on the other, the following regulations have been agreed upon:

ARTICLE 1. The vessels and ships of war of the parties at war shall be admitted to the Kingdom's sea channels, mentioned in article 1 of the royal order of February 2, 1893 (Official Gazette No. 46), with due observance of the further provisions of that order, for a sojourn not exceeding twenty-four hours, unless it is absolutely necessary that a longer sojourn be granted them, either for the procuring of provender or coal, or in case of distress or dangers of the sea.

In these cases, however, they shall leave as soon as the shipment of provender or coal has been effected, which, if possible, shall be done within the first twenty-four hours, and, if not, then as quickly as possible, as soon as the dangers of the sea are passed or in case of repairs at latest within twenty-four hours after they have been effected.

In any other case the length of the sojourn shall not exceed twenty-four hours, except it becomes necessary in the carrying out of the provision of article 5 of this proclamation.

Provender may be shipped so far as is necessary for the wants of the crew, while the store of coal shall only be supplemented sufficiently to allow the ship or vessel to reach the nearest port of the country to which it belongs, or that of one of its allies in the war.

The same ship may not be provided a second time with coal, except after a lapse of three months from the first lading, unless special permission be given.

ART. 2. Privateers shall not be admitted to Netherlands' ports or roads of sea channels, except in case of dangers of the sea, distress, or lack of provender.

As soon as the reason for their admittance has ceased to exist, they shall immediately move off.

They shall not be allowed to ship more provender than is necessary to permit of their reaching the nearest port of the country to which the ship belongs, or that of one of its allies in the war, and not more coal than is necessary to provide for their wants for twenty-four hours, sailing at a maximum pace of 10 English miles per hour.

Within a period of three months they shall not take in a fresh cargo of coal.

ART. 3. The ships of war or privateers of the parties at war shall not enter Netherlands' ports or sea channels with prizes, except in case of dangers of the sea or lack of provender.

As soon as the reason for their admittance has ceased to exist, they shall move off.

They shall not be allowed to ship more provender than is necessary to permit of their reaching the nearest port of the country to which the ship belongs, or that of one of its allies.

Coal shall not be supplied them so long as they are in possession of prizes.

If ships of war, pursued by the enemy, seek a refuge within our terrritory, they shall liberate the prizes.

ART. 4. The sale, exchange, and free disposal of prizes or of articles coming thence, as also of booty, is prohibited in the ports, roads, sea channels, and in the territorial waters of the Netherlands.

ART. 5. Ships and vessels of war, which in virtue of articles 1, 2, and 3 are admitted, shall not remain in our ports, roads, or sea channels beyond the time therein indicated.

If, however, war ships or other ships and vessels of the parties at war should simultaneously be in the same harbor, roads, or sea channel of the State, a period of twenty-four hours shall elapse between the departure of a ship or ships, of a vessel or vessels, of the one party and the departure of a ship or ships, of a vessel or vessels, of the other party.

This period, according to circumstances, may be extended by the local maritime authorities.

The above-mentioned ministers.

W. H. DE BEAUFORT.
CORT V. D. LINDEN.
RÖELL.
ELAND.

A royal order appearing in the Official Gazette of June 5, transmitted by Mr. Newel on June 6, prohibited the exportation and transit of ammunition and gunpowder from June 7, 1898. It will be observed, says Mr. Newel, that the prohibition is of a temporary nature; that it does not apply to the ordinary supply carried by trading vessels; and that exceptions thereto may be granted to goods destined to any country but those at war.

The order, after the usual preamble, reads:

ARTICLE 1. The exportation and transit of ammunition and gunpowder is forbidden.

This prohibition does not apply to the ammunition and gunpowder exported in the service of the State, nor to that which in a ship's service is found on board any Netherlands or foreign trading vessel, provided the supply on board does not exceed that usually carried by the sort of vessel in ordinary equipment.

ART. 2. Exception may be granted to this prohibition by the director of direct taxes, customs, and excise in whose district the place is situated whence the goods leave the Kingdom, to the sendings to the possessions of the Kingdom in other parts of the world, or to states which are not at war, provided the destination is satisfactorily shown him.

ART. 3. This order shall go into force on the second day after the date of the Official Gazette and of the Official Journal in which it is inserted.

NETHERLANDS INDIA.

Consul Everett, of Batavia, under date of April 29, 1898, sends copies of neutrality proclamations as printed in the Javasche Courant, as follows:

[From the Javasche Courant, April 26, 1898.]

When war broke out between Spain and the United States of North America, the Government of the Netherlands notified the belligerent powers of its intention to observe the strictest neutrality in this war.*

The government of the Dutch East Indies reminds the inhabitants of said Indies, and, so far as may be necessary, those who are in foreign countries, that they must abstain from any act that, being in violation of the laws of the Mother Country or of this colony, or of international law, might be considered as hostile to one of the belligerent powers or as not in harmony with strict neutrality.

It is enjoined upon them to respect an effective blockade and other measures of the belligerent powers that do not violate the laws of war, and to submit to the same, and they are not allowed to recruit soldiers or sailors for the armies and navies of said powers, to assist in the equipment of their war ships, or to supply or convey transports and contraband of war for them, or to engage in privateering or in the purchase and sale of booty.

The Government warns them that they may rely upon its protection and intervention only in case they, on their part, carefully refrain from any violation of the duties of neutrals; whereas if they neglect these duties, they render themselves liable to damages, difficulties, and prosecutions by the courts of the Netherlands, of the Dutch East Indies, or of foreign countries.

The Government, in conclusion, calls the attention of the inhabitants of the Dutch East Indies to article 100 of the penal code of the Netherlands, to articles 47 and 48 of the penal code in the Dutch East Indies for Europeans, and to articles 50 and 51 of the same code for natives.

[From the Javasche Courant, April 29, 1898.]

According to information received from the Minister of the Colonies, the Government of Spain and that of the United States of North America will adhere, during the war which has just broken out, to points 2, 3, and 4 of the declaration of Paris of April 16, 1856, and there will be no privateering for the present.

Points 2, 3, and 4 of the aforesaid declaration are as follows:

(2) The neutral flag protects the enemy's goods, except contraband of war.

(3) Neutral goods, except contraband of war, are not subject to seizure under the enemy's flag.

(4) Blockades, to be binding, must be effective, *i. e.*, maintained by a force sufficient to render approach to the enemy's coast really dangerous.

According to a communication from the Minister of the Colonies, information has been received from the Spanish Government that access to the ports of the Philippines is possible only with the help of the coast pilots who are available there,

---

* See p. 53.

because there is a possibility that the beacons have been removed and the coast lights extinguished.

In pursuance of instructions received from the governor-general, the (colonial) secretary-general notifies all whom it may concern that, for the maintenance of the strict neutrality during the war between Spain and the United States of North America which is mentioned in the warning contained in the Javasche Courant of April 26, 1898, the following rules have been laid down:

(1) No vessels of war or privateers belonging to a belligerent power shall be permitted to enter the ports or channels of the Dutch East Indies with prizes, or to remain there or in the roadsteads, except in cases of evident distress, such as disaster suffered at sea and lack of provisions. They shall leave at once when the cause of their stay has ceased.

(2) The sale, exchange, or donation of any prizes or of articles that have belonged thereto, and of goods that have been captured, is prohibited in the ports or channels of the Dutch East Indies. Further, the unrigging and the sale of vessels of war or cruisers of the belligerents are prohibited in the aforesaid ports, and also the unrigging and sale of privateers (provided that the latter are admitted).

(3) Privateers, even without prizes, shall not be permitted to enter the ports or channels of the Dutch East Indies, except in the cases mentioned sub numero 1, the concluding portion of which is applicable to them. They shall not be allowed to take in more provisions than are required for their immediate use; they may take in only as much coal as is necessary to supply their wants for twenty-four hours; and, so far as the same vessel is concerned, not more than once in three months.

(4) The vessels of war of the belligerent parties shall, provided that they submit to the rules of international law which govern their admission to neutral ports, be allowed to remain for not more than forty-eight hours, and not more than two vessels of each belligerent party shall be allowed to remain at the same time in ports of the Dutch East Indies; they shall be allowed to procure provisions and such quantity of coal as they may require to reach the nearest port of the country to which the ship belongs. No assistance shall, however, be rendered such vessels for making repairs or improvements, nor shall any materials necessary for such purposes be furnished to them.

(5) When vessels of the belligerent parties (whether vessels of war, privateers, or merchantmen) are simultaneously in the same port, roadstead, or in the territorial waters of the Dutch East Indian possessions, a period of at least twenty-four hours must elapse between the departure of a vessel belonging to one belligerent party and the subsequent departure of a vessel belonging to the other party. This period of time may be extended by the port authorities, according to circumstances.

(6) The furnishing of arms or ammunition to vessels of war of the belligerent parties is prohibited, and it is further prohibited to render them assistance in any way in increasing their crews, armament, or equipment.

BUITENZORG, *April 28, 1898.*

A. D. H. HERINGA,
Secretary-General.

Under date of June 13, Consul Everett, of Batavia, transmits copy and translation of neutrality circulars issued by the Netherlands colonial authorities. The orders, with the exception of the introductory phrases, are the same as those issued by the Netherlands,* with the exception of paragraph *d* in the first colonial circular,

---
*See p. 53.

which differs from paragraph *d* in the corresponding home circular in that it refers to provisions of the penal code for the Netherlands India, in addition to certain sections of the penal code of the Netherlands. The paragraph in the colonial circular reads:

(*d*) [It is prohibited] to volunteers to organize themselves in a military way within the territory of the State, with the intent to join the army of either of the belligerents.

And the secretary-general further refers to sections 100, 388, and 389 of the Dutch penal code, sections 47 and 48 of the penal code of Netherlands India for Europeans, and sections 50 and 51 of the penal code for natives; and by these presents warns all residents not in any way whatsoever to take a hand in privateering, and not to accept foreign letters of marque; as any persons who exercise privateering by virtue of such documents, or who in any way assist in so doing, will be prosecuted before the courts of justice.

NICARAGUA.

Minister Merry, in an inclosure dated San José, May 14, 1898, sends the following note from the Minister of Foreign Relations of Nicaragua:

MANAGUA, *April 30, 1898.*

Hon. WILLIAM L. MERRY,
 San José, Costa Rica:

I acknowledge the receipt of Your Excellency's telegram dated yesterday, which serves to inform my Government that a state of war has been declared by North America with the Kingdom of Spain, from the 21st of the present month. Regretting the painful situation between two civilized countries, I declare the absolute neutrality of the Nicaraguan Government in the conflict alluded to.

I am, etc.,

ERASMO CALDERON.

PARAGUAY.

Under date of May 12, 1898, Minister Finch sends from Montevideo copy of a telegram received from the Minister of Foreign Affairs of Paraguay, as follows:

ASUNCION, *May 10, 1898.*

To WILLIAM R. FINCH,
 Minister, Montevideo.

Yesterday I had the honor to receive Your Excellency's note, dated April 26 ultimo, communicating that a state of war exists between the United States and Spain; and I hasten to make known to Your Excellency, in accordance with the wishes and instructions of the President of the Republic, that the Government of Paraguay, faithful to its international duties, will maintain the strictest neutrality during the said conflict.

JOSÉ DECOUD.

PERU.

Minister Dudley transmits from Lima, under date of April 29, 1898, translation of a note from the Minister of Foreign Relations, as follows:

> FOREIGN OFFICE,
> *Lima, April 27, 1898.*
>
> Mr. MINISTER: I have had the honor to receive the esteemed note of yesterday's date, that, in obedience to instructions received from Washington, Your Excellency has been pleased to address me, in order to inform my Government of the late resolution of the American Congress, approved by His Excellency President McKinley, declaring that a state of war exists and has existed between the United States of America and Spain from the 21st instant.
>
> My Government having attentively watched the development of events, the unfortunate conclusion of which Your Excellency announces to me, is pained to receive the notification of war declared between two great nations allied to our own by ties of friendship, and heartily desires the prompt conclusion of the struggle just begun, and will comply with the duty imposed upon it by observing the rights and obligations of a state of neutrality.
>
> I am pleased to renew to Your Excellency the expressions of my high and distinguished consideration.
>
> E. DE LA RIVA-AGÜERO.

PORTUGAL.

Minister Townsend sends from Lisbon, under date of April 29, 1898, copy of the official announcement of neutrality by the Portuguese Government. A copy of the announcement, together with the order governing the use of the cable service with Madeira and the Azores, had been transmitted by the Portuguese minister at Washington under date of May 14. The translation, made in the Department of State, reads:

War having been declared between the Kingdom of Spain and the Republic of the United States of America, and it being desirable that the friendly relations and good understanding now existing between Portugal and other governments should be maintained and unalterably preserved by the observance on our part of the strictest and most absolute neutrality toward both the belligerent powers:

In view of paragraph 15 of article 75 of the constitution of the Monarchy; of the decrees of August 30, 1780; of June 3, 1803; of May 5, 1854; of July 29, 1861; of July 2, 1866; and of July 28, 1870; of articles 148, 150, 154, 155, 156, and 162 of the penal code; of the principles set forth in the declaration of Paris of April 16, 1856, made by the representatives of the powers that signed the treaty of peace of March 30 of the same year, to which Portugal gave her adhesion on the 28th of July following, and also of the doctrine generally received respecting the rights and duties of neutrals:

After having heard the Council of State, I have seen fit to decree the following:

ARTICLE 1. Portuguese subjects and aliens are forbidden to arm or fit out vessels intended for privateering, in the ports or waters of this Kingdom, whether on the Continent, the adjacent islands, or in the Portuguese colonies beyond the sea.

ART. 2. The entrance into the ports and waters mentioned in the foregoing article, of privateers and prizes taken by them or by any vessels of war of the belligerent powers is likewise forbidden.

Sole paragraph.—Cases of vis major, in which, according to international law, hospitality becomes indispensable, are excepted from the provisions of this article, but the sale of articles obtained from prizes shall not be allowed, and vessels having charge of prizes shall not be permitted to remain for a longer time than is indispensable for them to receive the necessary aid.

ART. 3. The entrance into the ports and waters mentioned in article 1 of vessels belonging to either of the belligerents, not having charge of prizes, and their stay there for a short time, shall be permitted, provided that such vessels conform to the rules laid down in the following paragraphs:

Paragraph 1.—War ships belonging to either of the belligerent powers shall not commit any act of hostility in the ports or waters of Portugal against the vessels or subjects of any other power, even of that of which the nation to which they belong is at war.

Paragraph 2.—The vessels aforesaid shall not be allowed to increase their crews in the aforesaid ports and waters by recruiting seamen of any nation, even of that to which the vessels belong.

Paragraph 3.—The aforesaid vessels are likewise forbidden to increase, within the said ports or waters, the number or caliber of their guns, or to receive on board portable arms or munitions of war.

Paragraph 4.—The aforesaid vessels shall not be allowed to leave port within twenty-four hours after the departure of any vessel belonging to another power with which the power to which they belong is at war, unless they obtain exemption from the limit of time above mentioned from the competent authorities, and furnish the required guaranties that they will not take advantage of that circumstance to commit any act of hostility against the hostile vessel.

ART. 4. The conveyance is permitted, under the Portuguese flag, of all articles of lawful commerce belonging to the subjects of either of the belligerent powers, and the conveyance is likewise permitted of articles of lawful commerce, belonging to Portuguese subjects, under the flag of either of the belligerent powers.

Paragraph 1.—Articles that may be considered as contraband of war are expressly excluded from the provision of this article.

Paragraph 2.—The provision of this article does not, moreover, apply to the ports of either of the belligerent powers that are in a state of effective blockade.

ART. 5. Portuguese subjects, and aliens resident in Portugal and its dominions, must abstain from all acts considered by the laws as calculated to jeopardize external security and opposed to the interests of the State in its relations with foreign nations.

ART. 6. The Government will not grant protection of any kind, from the acts or measures of belligerents, to Portuguese subjects or to any others who shall fail to observe the provisions of this decree. The provision of this article shall not invalidate any criminal proceedings that may be instituted according to laws now in force.

Let the President of the Council of Ministers, Minister and Secretary of State of the Affairs of the Kingdom, and the Ministers and Secretaries of State in charge of the other Departments so understand and cause it to be executed.

THE KING.
JOSÉ LUCIANO DE CASTRO.
FRANCISCO ANTONIO DA VEIGA BEIRÃO.
FREDERICO RESSANO GARCIA.
FRANCISCO MARIA DA CUNHA.
FRANCISCO FELISBERTO DIAS COSTA.
HENRIQUE DE BARROS GOMES.
AUGUSTO JOSÉ DA CUNHA.

Done at the palace, this 28th day of April, 1898.

DIRECTION OF THE TELEGRAPHIC AND POSTAL SERVICES,
DEPARTMENT OF TELEGRAPHS.

It is announced by superior order that, at the semaphoric stations on the Continent, the Azores and Madeira, the telegraphic sea-notice service has been discontinued (to which reference is made in articles 274, 275, 276, 277, and 278 of the regulations relative to telegraphic correspondence of December 10, 1892) as regards that portion of it which relates to the appearance, entrance, and departure of war vessels of all nationalities; but the other semaphoric services mentioned in articles 265 to 273 of the said regulation and in articles 62 and 63 of the international telegraphic regulations (Budapest revision) will be continued.

Direction of the Telegraphic and Postal Services, April 27, 1898.

For the Director-General of Posts and Telegraphs.

ALFREDO PEREIRA.

ROUMANIA.

Under date of Bucharest, May 17, 1898, Minister Rockhill incloses the declaration of neutrality of Roumania, as follows:

[Translation.]

In consequence of the communications received from the Government of the United States of North America and the Kingdom of Spain, the following declaration approved by His Majesty the King is published:

The Government of His Majesty the King of Roumania brings to the public knowledge that it will observe the strictest neutrality during the war between Spain and the United States of North America.

The Government of His Majesty the King particularly calls on this occasion the attention of all citizens of the Kingdom to the fact that, conformably to the above declaration, they must abstain from all acts which might be considered as hostile to either one of the belligerent States, and that it is specially forbidden them by law to enlist, in whatever capacity it may be, in their armies, as it is also forbidden them to contribute to the arming or equipping of a ship of war.

RUSSIA.

Ambassador Hitchcock sends from St. Petersburg, under date of May 3, 1898, translation of a note from the Ministry of Foreign Affairs, as follows:

MINISTRY OF FOREIGN AFFAIRS,
SECOND DEPARTMENT,
St. Petersburg, April 20 (May 2), 1898.

Mr. AMBASSADOR: I have the honor to inform you that His Majesty the Emperor, my August Master, by an order to the Acting Senate, dated April 18, has deigned to command that the following declaration of neutrality which the Imperial Government has resolved to observe in the Spanish-American conflict be made generally known:

"The disagreements which have recently arisen between Spain and the United States of America have induced the Imperial Government to seek, in concert with the other powers, some means which might prevent an armed conflict between these two countries.

"Unhappily, our friendly measures are without result, and a state of war now exists between Spain and the United States.

"It is with keen regret that the Imperial Government witnesses an armed conflict between two States to which it is united by old friendship and deep sympathy. It is firmly resolved to observe with regard to these two belligerents a perfect and impartial neutrality.

"The Imperial Government has taken note of the declarations of the Spanish and American Governments relative to their intention to conform, during the entire duration of the war, to the following generally recognized principles of international law:

"(1) The neutral flag covers the enemy's goods, except contraband of war.

"(2) Neutral goods, except contraband of war, are not liable to capture under the enemy's flag.

"(3) A blockade, to be obligatory, must be effective.

"All subjects of His Majesty the Emperor, as well as all persons under the protection of the laws of the Empire, are looked to to fulfill the obligations which a state of neutrality requires. Those who violate these provisions will be answerable before the law and can in no case receive aid or protection from the Imperial Government or its diplomatic and consular agents abroad.

"The Imperial Government further declares, that the ships of war of the two belligerent powers may only enter Russian ports for twenty-four hours. In case of stress of weather, absence of goods or provisions necessary to the maintenance of the crew, or for indispensable repairs, the prolongation of the above-mentioned time can only be accorded by special authorization of the Imperial Government.

"In case of ships of the two belligerents entering a Russian port, the merchant ship or the ship of war of one of the belligerent parties may leave the port only twenty-four hours after the ship of the other party shall have quitted the same port.

"The sale of prizes is absolutely forbidden in Russian ports."

Please to accept, etc.,

COUNT MOURAVIEFF.

SALVADOR.

The following has been received from Minister Merry, under date of San José, May 14, 1898:

SAN SALVADOR, *May 12.*

Señor MERRY,
United States Minister, San José.

Salvador, Honduras, and Nicaragua are the three countries which form the Greater Republic of Central America, recognized by all the countries of Europe and America, and, as you know already, the Diet is composed of the respective delegates who act in Managua, representing the transient sovereignty of the States mentioned, and consequently having charge of their foreign relations. For this reason the Government of Salvador, as well as Honduras and Nicaragua, have no minister of foreign relations, by virtue of which, in answering the information in your telegram of April 30 ultimo, notifying this Government of the state of war between the United States and Spain, for which attention I am much obliged, I do so in personal form, not having the faculty according to diplomatic usage, for the reasons which I have explained.

With protests, etc.,

P. ALFARO,
Minister of the Interior, Charged with Foreign Relations.

SERVIA.

The Department has received from Minister Rockhill, under date of Bucharest, May 16, 1898, translation of a note from the Minister of Foreign Affairs of Servia, as follows:

BELGRADE, *April 30, 1898.*

Mr. MINISTER: By note of the 26th instant, Your Excellency was pleased to inform the Royal Government that a state of war existed between the United States of America and Spain since the 21st instant, the day on which the Spanish Government informed the minister of the United States at Madrid that it considered the joint resolution of Congress, approved the 20th instant, as equivalent to a declaration of war, and that it had consequently recalled its minister from Washington and broken off diplomatic relations.

Your Excellency desires to be assured as to the neutrality of Servia during the war which has broken out.

While thanking Your Excellency most earnestly for his obliging communication, the Royal Government gives the assurance that Servia will observe, during the war which has broken out between the United States of North America and Spain, the strictest neutrality.

Please accept, etc.,

VLADAN GEORGEVITCH.

SIAM.

Under date of May 10, 1898, Minister King sends from Bangkok copy of a note from the Minister of Foreign Affairs, as follows:

FOREIGN OFFICE, *April 30, 1898.*

Mr. MINISTER: I have the honor to acknowledge receipt of the letter of your predecessor dated the 23d instant and of your letter dated the 27th instant. In his letter of the 23d Mr. Barrett, in accordance with instructions of the Secretary of State of the United States, notified me that, by proclamation issued on the 22d instant, under resolutions of Congress, duly approved on the 20th instant, His Excellency the President of the United States announces a blockade of the coast on the north side of Cuba between Cardenas and Bahia Honda; also Cienfuegos on the south side.

Mr. Barrett also informs me that, according to a later dispatch received by you, the United States Government, in the event of hostilities breaking out between that country and Spain, will not resort to privateering, but will follow the recognized rules of international law with regard to maritime trade.

Finally, in your letter of the 27th instant, you inform me that, by an act approved by the President on the 26th of April, the United States Congress has declared that a state of war exists between the United States and Spain since and including April 21.

I have taken due notice of these several communications, which I laid before His Majesty the King, my August Sovereign, and I am directed to say in reply that, according to the wish expressed by you in the name of your Government, His Majesty's Government will assume a strict neutrality during the existing war.

I avail myself of this occasion to express to you, Mr. Minister, the assurance of my high consideration.

DEVAWONGSE,
Minister for Foreign Affairs.

ST. LUCIA.

Consular Agent Peter sends through Consul Macallister, of the Barbados, under date of April 29, 1898, copy of the St. Lucia Gazette Extraordinary of April 25, which publishes in brief the rules in regard to foreign enlistment and the treatment of ships of belligerents contained in the proclamation of Great Britain.*

STRAITS SETTLEMENTS.

The Straits Settlements Government Gazette, April 25, 1898 (transmitted by Consul-General Pratt, of Singapore, on the same date), quotes the rules governing ships of belligerents and the terms

---

* See p. 31.

of the foreign enlistment act, as given in the proclamation of Great Britain,* and adds:

In order that the above rules may be duly carried out and respected, it is hereby notified that no ship of war of either of the belligerent parties above mentioned will be permitted to receive from any person or body corporate any commodity, including also stores, necessaries, and coal, without permission first obtained in writing from the master attendant or harbor master of the port.

SWEDEN AND NORWAY.

The following, dated Stockholm, April 26, 1898, has been received from Minister Thomas:

I have the honor to inform the Department that I have this evening received a note from the Minister for Foreign Affairs, in which he states that—

His Majesty the King, my August Sovereign, in view of the hostilities between the United States and Spain, has decided to observe for the United Kingdom a strict neutrality.

SWITZERLAND.

The Department has received the following from Minister Leishman, of Berne, dated April 27, 1898:

I have the honor to inclose herewith copy and translation of a letter just received from President Ruffy, acknowledging receipt of my note of yesterday communicating to the Swiss Government the proclamation of the President declaring the existence of a state of war.

The translation reads:

BERNE, *April 27, 1898.*

Mr. MINISTER: By note of April 26, Your Excellency kindly informed us that a state of war between the United States and Spain commenced on April 21, the day on which the Spanish Government made known to the minister of the United States at Madrid that it would consider the resolution of Congress, approved on the 20th of April, equivalent to a declaration of war, and that it had accordingly withdrawn its minister from Washington and terminated diplomatic relations.

Your Excellency desires to be assured with regard to the neutrality of the Swiss Government during the war which has just broken out.

In thanking Your Excellency most warmly for these kind communications, the Federal Council gives you the assurance that Switzerland, faithful to her traditions, will observe in the war which has just broken out between the United States and Spain the strictest neutrality.

Please accept, etc.,

In the name of the Swiss Federal Council,
The President of the Confederation,
RUFFY.
The Chancellor of the Confederation,
RINGIER.

---

*See p. 31.

TURKEY.

Minister Angell, in a dispatch from Constantinople of April 25, 1898, reporting an interview with the Turkish Minister for Foreign Affairs, says:

He (the Minister for Foreign Affairs) assured me that the Ottoman Empire would maintain a strict neutrality between Spain and the United States in the case of hostilities.

URUGUAY.

The Department has received a note from Mr. de Murguiondo, consul-general of Uruguay, dated Washington, June 10, 1898, transmitting a communication from the Minister of Foreign Affairs of Uruguay, which is translated as follows:

MINISTRY OF FOREIGN AFFAIRS,
Montevideo, May 4, 1898.

Mr. CONSUL-GENERAL: I beg to acknowledge receipt of your note of March 24.

A state of war having been unfortunately established between Spain and North America, the Government of Uruguay has determined to maintain strict neutrality in this armed struggle.

With salutations,

J. DE SALTEVANI.

Minister Finch writes from Montevideo, May 17, 1898:

I wish to call attention to the attitude of Uruguay in reference to the enforcement of neutrality. On receipt of the telegram from the Secretary of State announcing a state of war, I notified the Minister of Foreign Affairs, and received a cordial note in response, in which the minister communicated the President's determination to enforce neutrality. The determination has been energetically carried out. Spanish residents (the colony of which numbers about 70,000) have tried more than once to have entertainments to raise funds for Spain, but the Government not only refused to permit the entertainments, but confiscated the subscription lists, eliciting severe criticism on the part of the pro-Spanish press. In response to an inquiry from me as to whether United States men-of-war would be allowed to enter this harbor and take coal and provisions, the answer was prompt and in the affirmative; and I was also assured that the Uruguayan Government would take reasonable precautionary measures to insure the safety of United States men-of-war while sojourning here. A guard has also been placed near the United States legation in Montevideo. President Cuestas, nearly every member of his cabinet, and an intelligent class of professional and business men are friendly to the United States.

VENEZUELA.

The following note addressed by the Government of Venezuela to the United States minister at Caracas (transmitted by Mr. Loomis under date of May 2, 1898) proclaims and defines the attitude of neutrality adopted by that country in the present conflict between the United States and Spain:

UNITED STATES OF VENEZUELA,
MINISTRY OF FOREIGN AFFAIRS,
Caracas, April 29, 1898.

YOUR EXCELLENCY: With your courteous communication of the 26th instant, Your Excellency inclosed a copy of a telegram received the same day from His Excellency the Secretary of State, in regard to the state of war existing since the 21st of the present month between the North American Republic and the Kingdom of Spain.

Inasmuch as His Excellency the Secretary of State, in communicating the fact of the existence of war, asked you to inform this Government, to the end that its neutrality might be assured, I have the honor to inform you that this expectation on the part of the Government of the United States is in perfect accord with the intentions of the Executive: to wit, that the Republic will preserve the strictest neutrality during the contest. The Government of Venezuela, through its regular channel, will to-day likewise inform the Spanish nation.

I renew, etc.,

J. CALCAÑO MATHIEU.

Minister Loomis writes from Caracas, June 7, 1898:

The Spanish vice-consul at Ciudad Bolivar having published in the newspapers a notice to the effect that there was open in his office a register wherein would be entered the names of all Spanish subjects who might desire voluntarily to aid, either with their persons or with their money, the Government of Spain in its war with the United States, the Venezuelan Government issued the following decree:

MINISTRY OF FOREIGN AFFAIRS,
UNITED STATES OF VENEZUELA,
DEPARTMENT OF FOREIGN PUBLIC LAW,
Caracas, June 1, 1898.

Resolved: The neutrality of Venezuela in the present war between the United States of America and the Kingdom of Spain having been communicated officially to the two belligerent nations through their diplomatic representatives in Caracas since the 29th of April, the President of the Republic deems it imperative, in view of the fact that there is no special neutrality law in existence, to call attention to the laws of the country in regard to this subject, in order that the authorities may see to the strict observance of those rules which are to guide the Republic in this international conflict.

Article 121 of the penal code now in force forbids "anyone, without authority from the National Government, from making levies or arming and equipping Venezuelans or foreigners on Venezuelan soil, destined for the service of another nation;" article 461 of said code likewise prohibits "any individual from arrogating to himself illegal functions, and, without authority, opening offices for making subscriptions or enlistments." Furthermore, article 151 of the federal constitution provides that "the prescriptions of the law of nations form part of the national legislation," and, as these impose upon the neutral state the obligation to abstain completely, directly or indirectly, from whatever concerns military operations, the President of the Republic enjoins upon the authorities the strictest vigilance to prevent any operation or public act on Venezuelan soil, in regard to expeditions or enlistments of any kind whatsoever, for either of the two belligerent nations.

Let this be communicated to the presidents of the States, governors of the district and federal territories, through the medium of the Ministry of Interior.

For the National Executive.

J. CALCAÑO MATHIEU.

Minister Loomis sends, under date of June 11, 1898, copy and translation of another decree of the Venezuelan Government in regard to neutrality. This decree was issued the more effectually to assure the neutrality of Venezuela against the attempt of Spanish subjects and sympathizers to carry out plans for aiding Spain in the present conflict by holding public meetings and opening offices for the subscription of money and the enlistment of men in the cause of Spain. The decree, translated, reads:

It having already been announced that the attitude of the United States of Venezuela in the present war between the United States of America and Spain is that of strict neutrality, the constitutional President of the United States of Venezuela decrees:

ARTICLE 1. That all the federal and State authorities shall exercise the strictest vigilance in their respective jurisdictions to prevent the accomplishment of any act contrary to neutrality, such as the enlistment of men, the collection of arms, the formation of clubs, the fitting out of expeditions, etc.

ART. 2. As to the commerce of Venezuela with the belligerents, it is limited by the prohibition to carry contraband of war, this including the transportation of correspondence and persons engaged in military service; also by the prohibition to violate established blockades when personal warning has been given by the commanders of the ships engaged in making said blockades effective.

§ In accordance with the rules proclaimed by the belligerents, and in conformity with the treaty law of Venezuela, enemy's goods under a neutral flag and neutral goods under the enemy's flag, except contraband of war, are not liable to capture or confiscation.

ART. 3. Venezuelans are forbidden to take out letters of marque if the belligerents adopt this method of warfare, which neither of the two has renounced.

ART. 4. Venezuelans who fail to respect these obligations or who in any way take part in the hostilities shall be subject to the consequences of their conduct, in accordance with national legislation, and to the penalties imposed upon them by the offended belligerent, and can not appeal to this Government for protection.

ART. 5. Vessels of war of the belligerents and privateers with prizes shall not be allowed to enter Venezuelan ports. They may, however, be allowed to enter in case of urgent necessity, after remedying which they must leave without delay.

ART. 6. This decree shall be communicated to those whom it may concern and be published.

Done, signed with my hand, sealed with the seal of the National Executive, and countersigned by the Minister of Foreign Affairs, in Caracas, the 6th day of June, 1898, eighty-seventh year of the independence and fortieth of the federation.

IGNACIO ANDRADE.

Countersigned:
   The Minister of Foreign Affairs,
      J. CALCAÑO MATHIEU.

Proclamations of the President relating to the War with Spain.

1. BLOCKADE OF CUBAN PORTS.
2. CALL FOR VOLUNTEERS.
3. WAR WITH SPAIN—MARITIME LAW.
4. SECOND CALL FOR VOLUNTEERS.
5. BLOCKADE———SOUTHERN CUBA AND SAN JUAN.
6. SUSPENSION OF HOSTILITIES.

Proclamations of the President relating to the War with Spain.

[Blockade of Cuban Ports.]

BY THE PRESIDENT OF THE UNITED STATES OF AMERICA:

A PROCLAMATION.

Whereas, by a joint resolution passed by the Congress and approved April 20, 1898, and communicated to the Government of Spain, it was demanded that said Government at once relinquish its authority and Government in the Island of Cuba, and withdraw its land and Naval forces from Cuba and Cuban waters; and the President of the United States was directed and empowered to use the entire land and Naval forces of the United States, and to call into the actual service of the United States the militia of the several States to such extent as might be necessary to carry said resolution into effect; and

Whereas, in carrying into effect said resolution, the President of the United States deems it necessary to set on foot and maintain a blockade of the North coast of Cuba, including all ports on said coast between Cardenas and Bahia Honda and the port of Cienfuegos on the South coast of Cuba:

Now, therefore, I, William McKinley, President of the United States, in order to enforce the said resolution, do hereby declare and proclaim that the United States of America have instituted, and will maintain a blockade of the North coast of Cuba, including ports on said coast between Cardenas and Bahia Honda and the port of Cienfuegos on the South coast of Cuba, aforesaid, in pursuance of the laws of the United States and the law of nations applicable to such cases. An efficient force will be posted so as to prevent the entrance and exit of vessels from the ports aforesaid. Any neutral vessel approaching any of said ports, or attempting to leave same, without notice or knowledge of the establishment of such blockade, will be duly warned by the Commander of the blockading forces, who will endorse on her register the fact, and the date, of such warning, where such endorsement was made; and if the same vessel shall again attempt to enter any blockaded port, she will be captured and sent to the nearest convenient port for such proceedings against her and her cargo as prize, as may be deemed advisable.

Neutral vessels lying in any of said ports at the time of the establishment of such blockade will be allowed thirty days to issue therefrom.

In witness whereof, I have hereunto set my hand and caused the seal of the United States to be affixed.

Done at the City of Washington, this 22d day of April, A. D. 1898, and of the Independence of the United States, the one hundred and twenty-second.

[SEAL.]

WILLIAM MCKINLEY

By the President.

JOHN SHERMAN
Secretary of State

[Call for Volunteers—Spain.]

BY THE PRESIDENT OF THE UNITED STATES,

A PROCLAMATION.

Whereas a joint resolution of Congress was approved on the twentieth day of April, 1898, entitled "Joint Resolution For the recognition of the independence of the people of Cuba, demanding that the Government of Spain relinquish its authority and government in the Island of Cuba, and to withdraw its land and naval forces from Cuba and Cuban waters, and directing the President of the United States to use the land and naval forces of the United States to carry these resolutions into effect," and

Whereas, by an act of Congress entitled "An Act to provide for temporarily Increasing the Military Establishment of the United States in time of war and for other purposes," approved April 22, 1898; the President is authorized, in order to raise a volunteer army, to issue his proclamation calling for volunteers to serve in the Army of the United States:

Now, therefore, I, William McKinley, President of the United States, by virtue of the power vested in me by the Constitution and the laws, and deeming sufficient occasion to exist, have thought fit to call forth and hereby do call forth, volunteers to the aggregate number of 125,000, in order to carry into effect the purpose of the said Resolution; the same to be apportioned, as far as practicable, among the several States and Territories and the District of Columbia, according to population, and to serve for two years, unless sooner discharged. The details for this object will be immediately communicated to the proper authorities through the War Department.

In witness whereof I have hereunto set my hand and caused the seal of the United States to be affixed.

Done at the city of Washington, this twenty-third day of April, A. D., 1898, and of the Independence of the United States the one-hundred and twenty-second.

[SEAL.]

WILLIAM MCKINLEY

By the President:
JOHN SHERMAN
Secretary of State

[War with Spain—Maritime Law.]

BY THE PRESIDENT OF THE UNITED STATES OF AMERICA:

A PROCLAMATION.

Whereas by an Act of Congress approved April 25, 1898, it is declared that war exists and that war has existed since the 21st day of April, A. D. 1898, including said day, between the United States of America and the Kingdom of Spain; and

Whereas, it being desirable that such war should be conducted upon principles in harmony with the present views of nations and sanctioned by their recent practice, it has already been announced that the policy of this Government will be not to resort to privateering, but to adhere to the rules of the Declaration of Paris;

Now, Therefore, I, William McKinley, President of the United States of America by virtue of the power vested in me by the Constitution and the laws, do hereby declare and proclaim:

1. The neutral flag covers enemy's goods, with the exception of contraband of war.

2. Neutral goods, not contraband of war, are not liable to confiscation under the enemy's flag.

3. Blockades in order to be binding must be effective.

4. Spanish merchant vessels, in any ports or places within the United States, shall be allowed till May 21, 1898, inclusive, for loading their cargoes and departing from such ports or places; and such Spanish merchant vessels, if met at sea by any United States ship, shall be permitted to continue their voyage, if, on examination of their papers, it shall appear that their cargoes were taken on board before the expiration of the above term; Provided, that nothing herein contained

shall apply to Spanish vessels having on board any officer in the military or naval service of the enemy, or any coal (except such as may be necessary for their voyage), or any other article prohibited or contraband of war, or any despatch of or to the Spanish Government.

5. Any Spanish merchant vessel which, prior to April 21, 1898, shall have sailed from any foreign port bound for any port or place in the United States, shall be permitted to enter such port or place, and to discharge her cargo, and afterward forthwith to depart without molestation; and any such vessel, if met at sea by any United States ship, shall be permitted to continue her voyage to any port not blockaded.

6. The right of search is to be exercised with strict regard for the rights of neutrals, and the voyages of mail steamers are not to be interfered with except on the clearest grounds of suspicion of a violation of law in respect of contraband or blockade.

In witness whereof, I have hereunto set my hand and caused the seal of the United States to be affixed.

Done at the City of Washington, on the twenty-sixth day of April, in the year of our Lord one thousand eight hundred and ninety-eight, and of the Independence of the United States the one hundred and twenty-second.

[SEAL.]

WILLIAM McKINLEY

By the President.
    ALVEY A. ADEE
        Acting Secretary of State.

[Second Call for Volunteers—Spain.]

BY THE PRESIDENT OF THE UNITED STATES,

A PROCLAMATION.

Whereas an Act of Congress was approved on the twenty-fifth day of April, 1898, entitled "An Act Declaring that war exists between the United States of America and the Kingdom of Spain", and

Whereas, by an Act of Congress entitled "An Act to provide for temporarily increasing the Military Establishment of the United States in time of war and for other purposes", approved April 22, 1898; the President is authorized, in order to raise a volunteer army, to issue his proclamation calling for volunteers to serve in the Army of the United States:

Now, Therefore, I, William McKinley, President of the United

States, by virtue of the power vested in me by the Constitution and the laws, and deeming sufficient occasion to exist, have thought fit to call forth and hereby do call forth, volunteers to the aggregate number of 75,000 in addition to the volunteers called forth by my proclamation of the twenty-third day of April, in the present year; the same to be apportioned, as far as practicable, among the several States and Territories and the District of Columbia, according to population, and to serve for two years, unless sooner discharged. The proportion of each arm and the details of enlistment and organization will be made known through the War Department.

In witness whereof I have hereunto set my hand and caused the seal of the United States to be affixed.

Done at the City of Washington, this twenty-fifth day of May, in the year of our Lord one thousand eight hundred and ninety-
[SEAL.] eight, and of the Independence of the United States the one hundred and twenty-second.

WILLIAM MCKINLEY

By the President:
WILLIAM R. DAY,
Secretary of State.

[Blockade—Southern Cuba and San Juan, Puerto Rico.]

BY THE PRESIDENT OF THE UNITED STATES:

A PROCLAMATION.

Whereas, for the reasons set forth in my Proclamation of April 22, 1898, a blockade of the ports on the northern coast of Cuba, from Cardenas to Bahia Honda, inclusive, and of the port of Cienfuegos, on the south cost of Cuba, was declared to have been instituted; and

Whereas, it has become desirable to extend the blockade to other Spanish ports:

Now therefore, I, William McKinley, President of the United States, do hereby declare and proclaim that, in addition to the blockade of the ports specified in my Proclamation of April 22, 1898, the United States of America has instituted and will maintain an effective blockade of all the ports on the south coast of Cuba, from Cape Frances to Cape Cruz, inclusive, and also of the port of San Juan, in the Island of Porto Rico.

Neutral vessels lying in any of the ports to which the blockade is by the present Proclamation extended, will be allowed thirty days to issue therefrom, with cargo.

In witness whereof, I have hereunto set my hand, and caused the Seal of the United States to be affixed.

Done at the City of Washington, this twenty-seventh day of June, A. D., 1898, and of the Independence of the United States the one hundred and twenty-second.

[SEAL.]

WILLIAM MCKINLEY

By the President:
J. B. MOORE,
Acting Secretary of State.

[Spain—Suspension of Hostilities.]

BY THE PRESIDENT OF THE UNITED STATES OF AMERICA:

A PROCLAMATION.

Whereas, by a protocol concluded and signed August 12th, 1898, by William R. Day, Secretary of State of the United States, and His Excellency Jules Cambon, Ambassador Extraordinary and Plenipotentiary of the Republic of France at Washington, respectively representing for this purpose the Government of the United States and the Government of Spain, the United States and Spain have formally agreed upon the terms on which negotiations for the establishment of peace between the two countries shall be undertaken; and

Whereas, it is in said protocol agreed that upon its conclusion and signature hostilities between the two countries shall be suspended, and that notice to that effect shall be given as soon as possible by each Government to the commanders of its military and naval forces:

Now, therefore, I, William McKinley, President of the United States, do, in accordance with the stipulations of the protocol, declare and proclaim on the part of the United States a suspension of hostilities, and do hereby command that orders be immediately given through the proper channels to the commanders of the military and naval forces of the United States to abstain from all acts inconsistent with this proclamation.

In witness whereof, I have hereunto set my hand and caused the seal of the United States to be affixed.

Done at the City of Washington, this 12th day of August, in the year of our Lord one thousand eight hundred and ninety-eight, and of the Independence of the United States, the one hundred and twenty-third.

[SEAL.]

WILLIAM MCKINLEY

By the President.
WILLIAM R. DAY
Secretary of State.

Orders of War and Navy Departments.

Orders of War and Navy Departments.

OCCUPATION OF SANTIAGO.

GENERAL ORDERS,
No. 101.

WAR DEPARTMENT,
ADJUTANT-GENERAL'S OFFICE,
Washington, July 18, 1898.

The following, received from the President of the United States, is published for the information and guidance of all concerned:

EXECUTIVE MANSION,
Washington, July 13, 1898.

To the Secretary of War.

SIR: The capitulation of the Spanish forces in Santiago de Cuba and in the eastern part of the Province of Santiago, and the occupation of the territory by the forces of the United States, render it necessary to instruct the military commander of the United States as to the conduct which he is to observe during the military occupation.

The first effect of the military occupation of the enemy's territory is the severance of the former political relations of the inhabitants and the establishment of a new political power. Under this changed condition of things the inhabitants, so long as they perform their duties, are entitled to security in their persons and property and in all their private rights and relations. It is my desire that the inhabitants of Cuba should be acquainted with the purpose of the United States to discharge to the fullest extent its obligations in this regard. It will therefore be the duty of the commander of the army of occupation to announce and proclaim in the most public manner that we come not to make war upon the inhabitants of Cuba, nor upon any party or faction among them, but to protect them in their homes, in their employments, and in their personal and religious rights. All persons who, either by active aid or by honest submission, cooperate with the United States in its efforts to give effect to this beneficent purpose will receive the reward of its support and protection. Our occupation should be as free from severity as possible.

Though the powers of the military occupant are absolute and supreme and immediately operate upon the political condition of the inhabitants, the municipal laws of the conquered territory, such as affect private rights of person and property and provide for the punishment of crime, are considered as continuing in force, so far as they are compatible with the new order of things, until they are suspended or superseded by the occupying belligerent and in practice they are not usually abrogated, but are allowed to remain in force and to be administered by the ordinary tribunals, substantially as they were before the occupation. This enlightened practice is, so far as possible, to be adhered to on the present occasion. The judges and the other officials connected with the administration of justice may, if they accept the supremacy of the United States, continue to administer the ordinary law of the land, as between man and man, under the supervision of the American commander in chief. The native constabulary will, so far as may be practicable, be preserved. The freedom of the people to pursue their accustomed occupations will be abridged only when it may be necessary to do so.

While the rule of conduct of the American commander in chief will be such as has just been defined, it will be his duty to adopt measures of a different kind, if, unfortunately, the course of the people should render such measures indispensable to the maintenance of law and order. He will then possess the power to replace or expel the native officials in part or altogether, to substitute new courts of his own constitution for those that now exist, or to create such new or supplementary tribunals as may be necessary. In the exercise of these high powers, the commander must be guided by his judgment and his experience and a high sense of justice.

One of the most important and most practical problems with which it will be necessary to deal is that of the treatment of property and the collection and administration of the revenues. It is conceded that all public funds and securities belonging to the government of the country in its own right, and all arms and supplies and other movable property of such government, may be seized by the military occupant and converted to his own use. The real property of the state he may hold and administer, at the same time enjoying the revenues thereof, but he is not to destroy it save in the case of military necessity. All public means of transportation, such as telegraph lines, cables, railways, and boats belonging to the state may be appropriated to his use, but unless in case of military necessity they are not to be destroyed. All churches and buildings devoted to religious worship and to the arts and sciences, all schoolhouses, are, so far as possible, to be protected, and all destruction or intentional defacement of such places, of historical monuments or archives, or of works of science or art, is prohibited, save when required by urgent military necessity.

Private property, whether belonging to individuals or corporations, is to be respected, and can be confiscated only for cause. Means of transportation, such as telegraph lines and cables, railways and boats, may, although they belong to private individuals or corporations, be seized by the military occupant, but unless destroyed under military necessity are not to be retained.

While it is held to be the right of the conqueror to levy contributions upon the enemy in their seaports, towns, or provinces which may be in his military possession by conquest and to apply the proceeds to defray the expenses of the war, this right is to be exercised within such limitations that it may not savor of confiscation. As the result of military occupation the taxes and duties payable by the inhabitants to the former government become payable to the military occupant, unless he sees fit to substitute for them other rates or modes of contribution to the expenses of the government. The moneys so collected are to be used for the purpose of paying the expenses of government under the military occupation, such as the salaries of the judges and the police, and for the payment of the expenses of the army.

Private property taken for the use of the army is to be paid for when possible in cash at a fair valuation, and when payment in cash is not possible, receipts are to be given.

All ports and places in Cuba which may be in the actual possession of our land and naval forces will be opened to the commerce of all neutral nations, as well as our own, in articles not contraband of war upon payment of the prescribed rates of duty which may be in force at the time of the importation.

WILLIAM MCKINLEY.

By order of the Secretary of War:

H. C. CORBIN,
Adjutant-General.

INSTRUCTIONS TO BLOCKADING VESSELS AND CRUISERS.

GENERAL ORDER } NAVY DEPARTMENT,
No. 492. } *Washington, June 20, 1898.*

The following "Instructions to Blockading Vessels and Cruisers," prepared by the Department of State, are published for the information and guidance of the naval service.

JOHN D. LONG,
Secretary.

INSTRUCTIONS TO BLOCKADING VESSELS AND CRUISERS.

1. Vessels of the United States, while engaged in blockading and cruising service, will be governed by the rules of international law, as laid down in the decisions of the courts and in the treaties and manuals furnished by the Naval Department to ships' libraries, and by the provisions of the treaties between the United States and other powers.

The following specific instructions are established for the guidance of officers of the United States:

BLOCKADE.

2. A blockade to be effective and binding must be maintained by a force sufficient to render ingress to or egress from the port dangerous. If the blockading vessels be driven away by stress of weather, but return without delay to their stations, the continuity of the blockade is not thereby broken; but if they leave their stations voluntarily, except for purposes of the blockade, such as chasing a blockade runner, or are driven away by the enemy's force, the blockade is abandoned or broken. As the suspension of a blockade is a serious matter, involving a new notification, commanding officers will exercise especial care not to give grounds for complaints on this score.

NOTIFICATIONS TO NEUTRALS.

3. Neutral vessels are entitled to notification of a blockade before they can be made prize for its attempted violation. The character of this notification is not material. It may be actual, as by a vessel of the blockading force, or constructive, as by a proclamation of the government maintaining the blockade, or by common notoriety. If a neutral vessel can be shown to have had notice of the blockade in any way, she is good prize and should be sent in for adjudication; but, should formal notice not have been given, the rule of constructive knowledge arising from notoriety should be construed in a manner liberal to the neutral.

4. Vessels appearing before a blockaded port, having sailed without notification, are entitled to actual notice by a blockading vessel. They should be boarded by an officer, who should enter in the ship's log the fact of such notice, such entry to include the name of the blockading vessel giving notice, the extent of the blockade, the date and place, verified by his official signature. The vessel is then to be set free; and should she again attempt to enter the same or any other blockaded port as to which she has had notice she is good prize.

5. Should it appear from a vessel's clearance that she sailed after notice of blockade had been communicated to the country of her port of departure, or after the fact of blockade had, by a fair assumption, become commonly known at that port, she should be sent in as a prize. There are, however, treaty exceptions to this rule, and these exceptions should be strictly observed.

6. A neutral vessel may sail in good faith for a blockaded port with an alternative destination to be decided upon by information as to the continuance of the blockade obtained at an intermediate port. But, in such case, she is not allowed to continue her voyage to the blockaded port in alleged quest of information as to the status of the blockade, but must obtain it and decide upon her course before she arrives in suspicious vicinity; and if the blockade has been formally established with due notification, any doubt as to the good faith of such a proceeding should go against the neutral and subject her to seizure.

7. In accordance with the rule adopted by the United States in the existing war with Spain, neutral vessels found in port at the time of the establishment of a blockade will, unless otherwise ordered by the United States, be allowed thirty days from the establishment of the blockade to load their cargoes and depart from such port.

8. A vessel under any circumstances resisting visit, destroying her papers, presenting fraudulent papers, or attempting to escape, should be sent in for adjudication. The liability of a blockade runner to capture and condemnation begins and terminates with her voyage. If there is good evidence that she sailed with intent to evade the blockade, she is good prize from the moment she appears upon the high seas. Similarly, if she has succeeded in escaping from a blockaded port she is liable to capture at any time before she reaches her home port. But with the termination of the voyage the offense ends.

9. The crews of blockade runners are not enemies and should be treated not as prisoners of war, but with every consideration. Any of the officers or crew, however, whose testimony before the prize court may be desired, should be detained as witnesses.

10. The men-of-war of neutral powers should, as a matter of courtesy, be allowed free passage to and from a blockaded port.

11. Blockade running is a distinct offense, and subjects the vessel attempting, or sailing with the intent, to commit it, to seizure, without regard to the nature of her cargo. The presence of contraband of war in the cargo becomes a distinct cause of seizure of the vessel, where she is bound to a port of the enemy not blockaded, and to which, contraband of war excepted, she is free to trade.

RIGHT OF SEARCH.

12. The belligerent right of search may be exercised without previous notice, upon all neutral vessels after the beginning of war, to determine their nationality, the character of their cargo, and the ports between which they are trading.

13. This right should be exercised with tact and consideration, and in strict conformity with treaty provisions, wherever they exist. The following directions are given, subject to any special treaty stipulations: After firing a blank charge, and causing the vessel to lie to, the cruiser should send a small boat, no larger than a whale boat, with an officer to conduct the search. There may be arms in the boat, but the men should not wear them on their persons. The officer, wearing only his side arms, and accompanied on board by not more than two men of his boat's crew, unarmed, should first examine the vessel's papers to ascertain her nationality and her ports of departure and destination. If she is neutral, and trading between neutral ports, the examination goes no further. If she is neutral, and bound to an enemy's port not blockaded, the papers which indicate the character of her cargo should be examined. If these show contraband of war the vessel should be seized;

if not, she should be set free, unless, by reason of strong grounds of suspicion, a further search should seem to be requisite.

14. Irrespective of the character of the cargo, or her purported destination, a neutral vessel should be seized if she—
(1) Attempts to avoid search by escape; but this must be clearly evident.
(2) Resists search with violence.
(3) Presents fraudulent papers.
(4) Is not supplied with the necessary papers to establish the objects of search.
(5) Destroys, defaces, or conceals papers.

The papers generally to be expected on board of a vessel are:
(1) The register.
(2) The crew list.
(3) The log book.
(4) A bill of health.
(5) A charter party.
(6) Invoices.
(7) Bills of lading.

15. A neutral vessel carrying hostile dispatches, when sailing as a dispatch vessel practically in the service of the enemy, is liable to seizure; but not when she is a mail packet and carries them in the regular and customary manner, either as a part of the mail in her mail bags, or separately, as a matter of accommodation and without special arrangement or remuneration. The voyages of mail steamers are not to be interfered with except on the clearest grounds of suspicion of a violation of law in respect of contraband or blockade.

16. A neutral vessel in the service of the enemy, in the transportation of troops or military persons, is liable to seizure.

MERCHANT VESSELS OF THE ENEMY.

17. Are good prize, and may be seized anywhere, except in neutral waters. To this rule, however, the President's proclamation of April 26, 1898, made the following exceptions:

"4. Spanish merchant vessels in any ports or places within the United States, shall be allowed till May 21, 1898, inclusive, for loading their cargoes and departing from such ports or places; and such Spanish merchant vessels, if met at sea by any United States ship, shall be permitted to continue their voyage, if, on examination of their papers, it shall appear that their cargoes were taken on board before the expiration of the above term; Provided that nothing herein contained shall apply to Spanish vessels having on board any officer in the military or naval service of the enemy, or any coal (except such as may be necessary for their voyage), or any other article prohibited or contraband of war, or any dispatch of or to the Spanish Government.

"5. Any Spanish merchant vessel which, prior to April 21, 1898, shall have sailed from any foreign port bound for any port or place in the United States, shall be permitted to enter such port or place, and to discharge her cargo, and afterward forthwith to depart without molestation; and any such vessel, if met at sea by any United States ship, shall be permitted to continue her voyage to any port not blockaded."

ENEMY'S PROPERTY IN NEUTRAL VESSELS NOT CONTRABAND OF WAR.

18. The President, by his proclamation of April 26, 1898, declared:
"1. The neutral flag covers enemy's goods, with the exception of contraband of war."

19. The term contraband of war comprehends only articles having a belligerent destination, as to an enemy's port or fleet. With this explanation, the following articles are, for the present, to be treated as contraband:

Absolutely contraband.—Ordnance; machine guns and their appliances, and the parts thereof; armor plate, and whatever pertains to the offensive and defensive armament of naval vessels; arms and instruments of iron, steel, brass, or copper, or of any other material, such arms and instruments being specially adapted for use in war by land or sea; torpedoes and their appurtenances; cases for mines, of whatever material; engineering and transport materials, such as gun carriages, caissons, cartridge boxes, campaigning forges, canteens, pontoons; ordnance stores; portable range finders; signal flags destined for naval use; ammunition and explosives of all kinds; machinery for the manufacture of arms and munitions of war; saltpeter; military accouterments and equipments of all sorts; horses.

Conditionally contraband.—Coal, when destined for a naval station, a port of call, or a ship or ships of the enemy; materials for the construction of railways or telegraphs, and money, when such materials or money are destined for the enemy's forces; provisions, when destined for an enemy's ship or ships, or for a place that is besieged.

SENDING IN OF PRIZES.

20. Prizes should be sent in for adjudication, unless otherwise directed, to the nearest home port, in which a prize court may be sitting.

21. The prize should be delivered to the court as nearly as possible in the condition in which she was at the time of seizure; and to this end her papers should be sealed at the time of seizure, and kept in the custody of the prize master. Attention is called to articles Nos. 16 and 17 for the government of the United States Navy. (Exhibit A.)

22. All witnesses, whose testimony is necessary to the adjudication of the prize, should be detained and sent in with her, and, if circumstances permit, it is preferable that the officer making the search should act as prize master.

23. As to the delivery of the prize to the judicial authority, consult sections 4615, 4616, and 4617, Revised Statutes of 1878. (Exhibit B.) The papers, including the log book of the prize, are delivered to the prize commissioners; the witnesses, to the custody of the United States marshal; and the prize itself remains in the custody of the prize master until the court issues process directing one of its own officers to take charge.

24. The title to property siezed as prize changes only by the decision rendered by the prize court. But, if the vessel itself, or its cargo, is needed for immediate public use, it may be converted to such use, a careful inventory and appraisal being made by impartial persons and certified to the prize court.

28. If there are controlling reasons why vessels may not be sent in for adjudication, as unseaworthiness, the existence of infectious disease, or the lack of a prize crew, they may be appraised and sold; and if this can not be done they may be destroyed. The imminent danger of recapture would justify destruction, if there was no doubt that the vessel was good prize. But, in all such cases, all the papers and other testimony should be sent to the prize court, in order that a decree may be duly entered.

EXHIBIT A.

ART. 16. No person in the Navy shall take out of a prize, or vessel seized as a prize, any money, plate, goods, or any part of her equipment, unless it be for the better preservation thereof, or unless such articles are absolutely needed for the use of any of the vessels or armed forces of the United States, before the same are adjudged lawful prize by a competent court; but the whole, without fraud, concealment, or embezzlement, shall be brought in, in order that judgment may be passed thereon; and every person who offends against this article shall be punished as a court-martial may direct.

ART. 17. If any person in the Navy strips off the clothes of, or pillages, or in any manner maltreats, any person taken on board a prize, he shall suffer such punishment as a court-martial may adjudge.

EXHIBIT B.

SEC. 4615. The commanding officer of any vessel making a capture shall secure the documents of the ship and cargo, including the log book, with all other documents, letters and other papers found on board, and make an inventory of the same, and seal them up, and send them, with the inventory, to the court in which proceedings are to be had, with a written statement that they are all the papers found, and are in the condition in which they were found; or explaining the absence of any documents or papers, or any change in their condition. He shall also send to such court, as witnesses, the master, one or more of the other officers, the supercargo, purser, or agent of the prize, and any person found on board whom he may suppose to be interested in, or to have knowledge respecting, the title, national character, or destination of the prize. He shall send the prize, with the documents, papers and witnesses, under charge of a competent prize master and prize crew, into port for adjudication, explaining the absence of any usual witnesses; and in the absence of instructions from superior authority as to the port to which it shall be sent, he shall select such port as he shall deem most convenient, in view of the interests of probable claimants, as well as of the captors. If the captured vessel, or any part of the captured property, is not in condition to be sent in for adjudication, a survey shall be had thereon and an appraisement made by persons as competent and impartial as can be obtained, and their reports shall be sent to the court in which proceedings are to be had; and such property, unless appropriated for the use of the Government, shall be sold by the authority of the commanding officer present, and the proceeds deposited with the assistant treasurer of the United States most accessible to such court, and subject to its order in the cause. (See sec. 1624, art. 15.)

SEC. 4616. If any vessel of the United States shall claim to share in a prize, either as having made the capture, or as having been within signal distance of the vessel or vessels making the capture, the commanding officer of such vessel shall make out a written statement of his claim, with the grounds on which it is founded, the principal facts tending to show what vessels made the capture, and what vessels were within signal distance of those making the capture, with reasonable particularity as to times, distances, localities, and signals made, seen, or answered; and such statement of claim shall be signed by him and sent to the court in which proceedings shall be had, and shall be filed in the cause.

SEC. 4617. The prize master shall make his way diligently to the selected port, and there immediately deliver to a prize commissioner the documents and papers, and the inventory thereof, and make affidavit that they are the same, and are in the same condition as delivered to him, or explaining any absence or change of condition therein, and that the prize property is in the same condition as delivered to him, or explaining any loss or damage thereto; and he shall further report to the district attorney and give to him all the information in his possession respecting the prize and her capture; and he shall deliver over the persons sent as witnesses to the custody of the marshal, and shall retain the prize in his custody until it shall be taken therefrom by process from the prize court. (See sec. 5441.)

War Decrees of Spain.

War Decrees of Spain.

The following is taken from the London Gazette of May 3, 1898, transmitted by Ambassador Hay, under date of May 4:

FOREIGN OFFICE, *May 3, 1898.*

The Secretary of State for Foreign Affairs has received, through Her Majesty's embassy at Madrid, the following translation of a decree issued by the Spanish Government on the 23d of April, 1898:

ROYAL DECREE.

In accordance with the advice of my Council of Ministers; in the name of my son, King Alfonso XIII, and as Queen-Regent of the Kingdom, I decree as follows:

ARTICLE. I. The state of war existing between Spain and the United States terminates the treaty of peace and friendship of the 27th October, 1795, the protocol of the 12th January, 1877, and all other agreements, compacts, and conventions that have been in force up to the present between the two countries.

ART. II. A term of five days from the date of the publication of the present royal decree in the Madrid Gazette is allowed to all United States ships anchored in Spanish ports, during which they are at liberty to depart.

ART. III. Notwithstanding that Spain is not bound by the declaration signed in Paris on the 16th April, 1856, as she expressly stated her wish not to adhere to it, my Government, guided by the principles of international law, intends to observe and hereby orders that the following regulations for maritime law be observed:

(*a*) A neutral flag covers the enemy's goods, except contraband of war.

(*b*) Neutral goods, except contraband of war, are not liable to confiscation under the enemy's flag.

(*c*) A blockade to be binding must be effective; that is to say, maintained with a sufficient force to actually prevent access to the enemy's coast.

ART. IV. The Spanish Government, while maintaining their right to issue letters of marque, which they expressly reserved in their note of the 16th May, 1857, in reply to the request of France for the adhesion of Spain to the declaration of Paris relative to maritime law, will organize for the present a service of "auxiliary cruisers of the navy," composed of ships of the Spanish mercantile navy, which will cooperate with the latter for the purposes of cruising, and which will be subject to the statutes and jurisdiction of the navy.

ART. V. In order to capture the enemy's ships, to confiscate the enemy's merchandise under their own flag, and contraband of war under any flag, the royal navy, auxiliary cruisers, and privateers, if and when the latter are authorized, will exercise the right of visit on the high seas and in the territorial waters of the enemy, in accordance with international law and any regulations which may be published for the purpose.

ART. VI. Under the denomination contraband of war, the following articles are included:

Cannons, machine guns, mortars, guns, all kinds of arms and firearms, bullets, bombs, grenades, fuses, cartridges, matches, powder, sulphur, saltpeter, dynamite and every kind of explosive, articles of equipment like uniforms, straps, saddles and artillery and cavalry harness, engines for ships and their accessories, shafts, screws, boilers and other articles used in the construction, repair, and arming of war ships, and in general all warlike instruments, utensils, tools, and other articles, and whatever may hereafter be determined to be contraband.

ART. VII. Captains, commanders, and officers of non-American vessels or of vessels manned as to one-third by other than American citizens, captured while committing acts of war against Spain, will be treated as pirates, with all the rigor of the law, although provided with a license issued by the Republic of the United States.

ART. VIII. The Minister of State and the Minister of Marine are charged to see the fulfillment of the present royal decree and to give the orders necessary for its execution.

MADRID, *April 23, 1898.* MARIA CRISTINA.

FOREIGN OFFICE, *May 3, 1898.*

The Secretary of State for Foreign Affairs has received through Her Majesty's embassy at Madrid the following translation of the instructions, drawn up by the Spanish Minister of Marine, for exercising the right of visit in accordance with article 5 of the royal decree which was issued on the 23d of April, 1898:

ROYAL ORDER.

YOUR EXCELLENCY: His Majesty the King, and in his name the Queen Regent, have been pleased to approve of the annexed instructions for exercising the right of visit. They have been drawn up by the Minister of Marine in accordance with article 5 of the royal decree issued by the President of the Council of Ministers on yesterday's date.

(Signed,) SEGISMUNDO BERMEJO.
MADRID, *April 24, 1898.*
To the President of the Council of the Fleet.

Instructions for the exercise of the right to visit.

1. Right of visit can only be exercised by belligerents; hence it can evidently be only resorted to during international conflicts by one or other of the states at war, as also during internal civil or insurrectionary wars, when one or more foreign powers have recognized the insurrectionary party as belligerents. In such circumstances, right of visit can be exercised by the Mother Country, but it is restricted to the merchant vessels of the nation or nations who have given this recognition, and who are for such reason in the position of neutrals.

2. In accordance with the position laid down in the preceding article, ships of war and merchant vessels of the belligerents, when legally armed either as auxiliary cruisers of their navy or as privateers, if and when they are authorized, may in their own territorial waters, or those under the jurisdiction of the enemy, or in the open seas, detain such merchant vessels as they meet with in order to verify the legitimacy of their flag, and, if neutrals, and proceeding to a port of the other belligerent, the nature of their cargo.

3. Seas subject to the sovereign jurisdiction of neutral powers are absolutely inviolable; right of visit may not, therefore, be resorted to within them, even if it be alleged that it was attempted to exercise such right in the open sea, and that, on

chase being given, and without losing sight of the vessel pursued, the latter penetrated into neutral waters.

Neither may the violation of the rights attaching to such waters be justified under the pretext that the coast washed thereby was undefended or uninhabited.

4. The following is the method of exercising right of visit:

(*a*) Notification to the vessel to be visited to lay to and state its nationality is made by the visiting vessel hoisting her national flag and firing a blank shot, a signal upon which the merchant vessel is bound to hoist the flag of the nation to which it belongs and lay to.

(*b*) If the merchant vessel does not obey this first intimation, and either refuses to hoist her flag or does not lay to, a second gun will be fired, this time loaded, care being taken that the shot does not strike the vessel, though going sufficiently close to her bows for the vessel to be duly warned; and if this second intimation be disregarded, a third shot will be fired at the vessel, so as to damage her, if possible, without sinking her. Whatever be the damage caused to the merchant vessel by this third shot, the commanding officer of the man-of-war or captain of the privateer can not be made responsible.

Nevertheless, in view of special circumstances, and in proportion to the suspicion excited by the merchantman, the auxiliary vessel of war or privateer may delay resorting to the last extremity until some other measure has been taken, such as not aiming the third discharge at the vessel, but approaching it and making a fresh notification by word of mouth; but if this last conciliatory measure prove fruitless, force will immediately be resorted to.

(*c*) The visiting vessel will place herself at such distance as her commander or captain may think convenient from the vessel to be visited, according to circumstances of wind, sea, current, or the suspicion inspired by the said vessel; and if these circumstances make it advisable for the boat about to make visit to approach on the windward side and go to leeward on returning, there is no reason why she should not do so.

But if, by existing treaties between the nations to which the vessels respectively belong, the distance to be kept is specified, such a clause of conventional law shall be respected, if the circumstances of wind, sea, or current above mentioned permit.

(*d*) The visiting vessel will send to the merchant vessel a boat with an officer, who will effect the visit in question, under a verbal commission from his commanding officer; said officer may board the merchant vessel in company with two or three of the crew of the boat, but it will be left to his discretion whether he shall do so or go alone.

(*e*) The visiting officer will inform the captain of the merchant vessel that, under commission from the commander of the Spanish ship of war, or of the auxiliary cruiser (here follows name of ship of war or auxiliary cruiser), or from the captain of the privateer (here follows name of vessel), he intends to effect a visit and will request him to produce his sailing papers, or official document which takes their place, in proof of the nationality of the vessel therein stated being that of the flag which he has hoisted, and to show the port to which the vessel is proceeding.

Should the first point be satisfactorily proved, and should the port of destiny prove to be a neutral one, the visit is thereby concluded.

But should the vessel be proceeding to a port belonging to the enemy of the nation to which the visiting vessel belongs, the officer will ask the captain of the merchant vessel for the documents in which the nature of the cargo is stated, in order to ascertain if there be contraband of war; should there be none, the visit is definitely concluded, and the neutral vessel is at liberty to proceed on its voyage; but should there be contraband, its capture is proceeded with, but no search may, in these circumstances, be made.

5. The visiting officer should have instructions from his commanding officer authorizing the visited vessel to continue her voyage, if the visit has presented no difficulties, in order that the delay may not be longer than is absolutely indispensable.

6. If the captain of the visited vessel asks to have the visit certified, the visiting officer will accede to his request and will insert a note in the sheet for the day in the ship's books in the following form:

The undersigned (rank in the navy), sailing on the (gunboat, cruiser, etc., of His Catholic Majesty, named ———, or the auxiliary cruiser or privateer), whose commanding officer is (rank and name), certifies that this day at (hour of morning or evening), under a verbal commission from the said commanding officer, has carried out the visit of the (class of vessel, name, and nationality of merchant service), captain (name of captain), and ascertained from the papers shown to him the legitimacy of the flag which she flies, and the neutrality of her cargo.

Date.

Signature of visiting officer.

Seal of visiting vessel.

7. The visit will likewise be recorded in the books of the visiting vessel, the following circumstances being stated:

(*a*) Details of the intimation or intimations given to the visited vessel.

(*b*) Hour of its laying to.

(*c*) Name and nationality of visited vessel and captain thereof.

(*d*) Manner in which visit was effected, and its result, stating name of officer who executed it.

(*e*) Hour at which vessel was authorized to proceed.

8. The record of the visit, which, as stated in Article VI, can be made at the wish of the captain of the visited vessel, will become an indispensable formality should the vessel contain wounded or sick soldiers, subjects of the enemy, for in such a case all such persons will, by the mere act of visit, be incapacitated from bearing arms again during the war, in accordance with the first paragraph of the tenth additional article of the Geneva Convention.

The visiting officer will therefore in such a case make a notification of the same to the chief of the expeditionary force, and will make a note in the books of the visited vessel in the form prescribed in Article VI, with the following addition:

This vessel contains (number of sick and wounded) individuals (of the army or navy or both) sick and wounded, subjects of the enemy, all of whom, by the fact of this visit, are incapacitated from bearing arms again during the war, according to paragraph one of the tenth additional article of the Geneva Convention, of which I have made notification to the commander of the expeditionary force, who stated that he was (here follow rank and name).

9. The visit is not an act of jurisdiction on the part of the belligerent; it is a natural means of legitimate defense allowed by international law, lest fraud and bad faith should assist the enemy. This right should therefore be exercised with the greatest moderation by the belligerent, special care being taken to avoid causing the neutral any extortion, damage, or trouble that is not absolutely justifiable.

In consequence of this, the detention of the ship visited should always be as short as possible, and the proceedings restricted as far as they can be, their exclusive object being, as explained, for the belligerent to ascertain the neutrality of the ship, and in case of its neutrality (if bound for a port of the enemy) the inoffensive and neutral description of its cargo.

It is not necessary, therefore, to demand during the visit any other documents than those proving these two conditions, for what the belligerent requires is to prevent any damage, favoring, or assisting the enemy; to prevent assistance and help being furnished to them that may contribute directly to the prolongation of the war, and not to be assured that all ships belonging to neutral powers are provided with all the documents required by the laws of their country.

10. In consequence of the visit the vessel is captured in the following case:

(1) If the nationality of the vessel proves to be that of the enemy, unless covered by the immunities established by the Geneva Convention by which Spain is bound. (The said exceptions are given at the end of these instructions.)

(2) If active resistance is offered to the visit, that is, if force is employed to escape it.

(3) If a legal document to prove the nationality can not be produced.

(4) If bound for the enemy's ports, the vessel can not produce a document proving the nature of the cargo.

(5) If the cargo is composed in whole or more than two-thirds of contraband of war.

In the case of the illicit part of the cargo being less than two-thirds only, the articles which are contraband of war will be confiscated, and to unload them the ship will be conducted to the nearest and most convenient Spanish port.

It must be understood that goods directly and immediately affecting the war are contraband only when destined for the enemy's ports, for when they are consigned to a neutral port these goods are munitions of war, but not contraband.

But if a vessel is dispatched for a neutral port in proper form, but makes for a port of the enemy, then, if found near to one of these ports or sailing in quite a different direction than the proper one shown in her papers, she shall be captured if the captain can not prove that force majeure drove him from his proper course.

(6) If she carries on behalf of the enemy officers, troops, or seamen.

(7) If she carries letters and communications of the enemy, unless she belong to a marine mail service, and these letters or communications are in bags, boxes, or parcels with the public correspondence, so that the captain may be ignorant of their contents.

(8) If the vessel is employed in watching the operations of the war, either freighted by the other belligerent or paid to perform this service.

(9) If the neutral vessel takes part in this employment, or assists in any way in such operations.

The vessel will also be captured when during the visit duplicate or false papers are found, since such cases fall under the regulations contained in clauses (3) and (4) or in both, since neither false nor duplicate papers can serve to justify the conditions referred to.

Neither an attempt at flight to escape visit, nor simple suspicion of fraud respecting the nationality of the vessel or the nature of its cargo, authorize the capture of the vessel.

The circumstance that the papers are written in a language unknown to the officer making the visit does not authorize the detention of the vessel.

11. Merchant vessels sailing under convoy, under charge of one or more ships of the navy of their nation, are absolutely exempt from the visit of the belligerents, being protected by the immunity enjoyed by the war ships.

As the formation of a convoy is a measure emanating from the government of the state to which belong the vessels protecting the convoy, as well as the vessels under convoy, it must be taken as certain that the government in question not only will not allow fraud of any kind, but has employed the strictest measures to avoid fraud being committed by any of the vessels under the convoy.

It is therefore useless for the belligerent to inquire of the chief officer of the convoy whether he guarantees the neutrality of the ships sailing under his charge, or of the cargo they carry.

12. On the visit taking place, it is not permissible to give orders to open the hatchways in order to examine the cargo, nor to open any article of furniture to search for documents. The ship's papers presented by the captain to prove the legitimacy of the flag and the nature of the cargo are the only proof which international law allows.

13. Although it very seldom occurs that the principal ship's papers, whether those referring to her nationality or to the nature of her cargo, are lost, mislaid, or left on shore by mistake, if such a case should occur, and by other papers or means the captain can convince the officer visiting the ship of the neutrality of the ship and her cargo, he may authorize the captain to continue her voyage; but if an explanation can not be given, the ship will be detained and conducted to the nearest Spanish port until the necessary investigation concerning the point or points in question is made.

14. The commander of the vessel carrying out the visit and the officer commissioned to make the visit, the former in ordering and the latter in carrying it out, should act without prejudice to the good faith of the neutral being visited, and without losing sight of the consideration and respect that nations owe to one another.

Note relative to the first section of Article X. The clauses of the Geneva Convention of the 22d August, 1864, and those of its additional articles drawn up at the second diplomatic conference of the 20th October, 1868, are as follows:

"*Articles concerning the marine.*

"ARTICLE VI.

"The boats which, at their own risk and peril, during and after an engagement, pick up the shipwrecked or wounded, or which, having picked them up, convey them on board a neutral or hospital ship, shall enjoy, until the accomplishment of their mission, the character of neutrality, as far as the circumstances of the engagement and the position of the ships engaged will permit.

"The appreciation of these circumstances is intrusted to the humanity of all the combatants. The wrecked and wounded thus picked up and saved must not serve again during the continuance of the war.

"ARTICLE VII.

"The religious, medical, and hospital staff of any captured vessel are declared neutral, and, on leaving the ship, may remove the articles and surgical instruments which are their private property.

"ARTICLE VIII.

"The staff designated in the preceding article must continue to fulfill their functions in the captured ship, assisting in the removal of the wounded made by the victorious party; they will then be at liberty to return to their country in conformity with the second paragraph of the first additional article.*

"The stipulations of the second additional article are applicable to the pay and allowance of the staff already mentioned.

"ARTICLE IX.

"The military hospital ships remain under martial law in all that concerns their stores; they become the property of the captor, but the latter must not divert them from their special appropriation during the continuance of the war.

---

*This article states that the time of departure will be fixed by the commander of the boarding party.

"ARTICLE X.

"Any merchantman, to whatever nation she may belong, charged exclusively with removal of sick and wounded, is protected by neutrality; but the mere fact, noted on the ship's books, of the vessel having been visited by an enemy's cruiser, renders the sick and wounded incapable of serving during the continuance of the war. The cruiser shall even have the right of putting on board an officer in order to accompany the convoy, and thus verify the good faith of the operation.

"If the merchant ship also carries a cargo, her neutrality will still protect it, provided that such cargo is not of a nature to be confiscated by the belligerents.

"The belligerents retain the right to interdict neutralized vessels from all communication, and from any course which they may deem prejudicial to the secrecy of their operations. In urgent cases special conventions may be entered into between commanders in chief, in order to neutralize temporarily and in a special manner the vessels intended for the removal of the sick and wounded.

"ARTICLE XI.

"Wounded or sick sailors and soldiers, when embarked, to whatever nation they may belong, shall be protected and taken care of by their captors.

"Their return to their own country is subject to the condition that they are bound not to bear arms again during the war.

"ARTICLE XII.

"The distinctive flag to be used with the national flag, in order to indicate any vessel or boat which may claim the benefits of neutrality, is a white flag with a red cross. The belligerents may exercise in this respect any mode of verification which they may deem necessary.

"Military hospital ships shall be distinguished by being painted white outside, with green strake.

"ARTICLE XIII.

"The hospital ships which are equipped at the expense of the aid societies, recognized by the signatory powers to the Geneva Convention, and which are furnished with a commission emanating from the sovereign, who shall have given express authority for their being fitted out, and with a certificate from the proper naval authority that they have been placed under his control until their final departure, and that they were then appropriated solely to the purpose of their mission, shall be considered neutral, as well as the whole of their staff. They shall be recognized and protected by the belligerents.

"They shall make themselves known by hoisting, together with their national flag, the white flag with a red cross. The distinctive mark of their staff, while performing their duties, shall be an armlet of the same colors. The outer painting of these hospital ships shall be white, with red strake.

"These ships shall bear aid and assistance to the wounded and wrecked belligerents, without distinction of nationality.

"They must take care not to interfere in any way with the movements of the combatants. During and after the battle they must do their duty at their own risk and peril.

"The belligerents shall have the right of controlling and visiting them; they will be at liberty to refuse their assistance, to order them to depart, and to detain them if the exigencies of the case require such a step.

"The wounded and wrecked picked up by these ships can not be reclaimed by either of the combatants, and they will be required not to serve during the continuance of the war.

"ARTICLE XIV.

"In naval wars any strong presumption that either belligerent takes advantage of the benefits of neutrality, with any other view than the interest of the sick and wounded, gives to the other belligerent, until proof to the contrary, the right of suspending the convention, as regards such belligerent."

The Minister of Marine,
(Signed,) SEGISMUNDO BERMEJO.

MADRID, *April 24, 1898.*

www.ingramcontent.com/pod-product-compliance
Lightning Source LLC
Chambersburg PA
CBHW020859160426
43192CB00007B/992